IS LIFE
SO DEAR ?

THE
NOBLE
ARMY OF
MARTYRS
PRAISE
THEE

AMERSHAM
MARTYRS.

IN THE SHALLOW DEPRESSION AT
A SPOT 100 YARDS LEFT OF THIS
MONUMENT, SEVEN PROTESTANTS, SIX MEN
AND ONE WOMAN WERE BURNED TO DEATH
AT THE STAKE. THEY DIED FOR THE
PRINCIPLES OF RELIGIOUS LIBERTY,
FOR THE RIGHT TO READ AND INTERPRET
THE HOLY SCRIPTURES AND TO WORSHIP
GOD ACCORDING TO THEIR CONSCIENCES
AS REVEALED THROUGH GOD'S HOLY WORD.

THEIR DEATHS SHALL LIVE FOR EVER.

WILLIAM TYLSWORTH. BURNED 1506.
JOAN CLARK, HIS MARRIED DAUGHTER, WAS
COMPELLED TO LIGHT THE FAGGOT TO BURN HER FATHER.

THOMAS BARNARD.   BURNED 1521.
JAMES MORDEN.   BURNED 1521.
JOHN SCRIVENER.   BURNED 1521,
HIS CHILDREN WERE COMPELLED TO LIGHT FAGGOTS TO BURN THEIR FATHER.

ROBERT RAVE.   BURNED 1521.
THOMAS HOLMES.   BURNED 1521.
JOAN NORMAN.   BURNED 1521.

THE FOLLOWING MEN, WORSHIPPERS AT
AMERSHAM, WERE MARTYRED IN
OTHER PLACES

ROBERT COSIN.
OF CLC WICOMBE BURNED IN BUCKINGHAM 1506.

THOMAS CHASE.
STRANGLED AT WOBURN 1506,
HIS BODY WAS BURIED AT WOBURN MOOR 1514.

THOMAS MAN.
BURNED AT SMITHFIELD 1518.

THOMAS HARDING.
BURNED AT CHESHAM 1532.

IS LIFE SO DEAR?

KEY ISSUES IN SPIRITUAL WARFARE

BROTHER ANDREW

Thomas Nelson Publishers
Nashville • Camden • New York

Published in Nashville, Tennessee, by Thomas Nelson, Inc. and distributed in Canada by Lawson Falle, Ltd., Cambridge, Ontario.

Printed in the United States of America.

Unless otherwise noted, all Scripture quotations are from the Revised Standard Version of the Bible, copyrighted 1946, 1952, © 1971, 1973 by the Division of Christian Education of the National Council of Churches of Christ in the U.S.A. and used by permission.

Scripture quotations noted KJV are from the King James Version of the Bible.

Scripture quotations noted NEB are from *The New English Bible.* © The Delegates of the Oxford University Press and the Syndics of the Cambridge University Press 1961, 1970. Reprinted by permission.

Scripture quotations noted NIV are from The Holy Bible: New International Version. Copyright © 1978 by the New York International Bible Society. Used by permission of Zondervan Bible Publishers.

Scripture quotations noted TLB are from *The Living Bible* (Wheaton, Illinois: Tyndale House Publishers, 1971) and are used by permission.

The excerpt from the article "To Smuggle or Not to Smuggle?" is reprinted by permission of *Christian Bookseller* magazine, copyright 1971, Christian Life Missions, 396 E. St. Charles Rd., Wheaton, Ill. 60188, and by the author.

The excerpt taken from *China: Christian Students Face the Revolution,* by David Adeney ©1973 by Inter-Varsity Christian Fellowship of the USA, is used by permission of InterVarsity Press, Downers Grove, Ill. 60515, and by the author.

Library of Congress Cataloging in Publication Data
Andrew, Brother.
  Is life so dear?

  Bibliography: p.161
  Includes index.
  1. Government, Resistance to Religious Aspects—
Christianity. 2. Persecution. I. Title.
BV630.2.A53   1985   241'.621   84-27344
ISBN 0-8407-5976-2

Second printing

Contents

Acknowledgements v
Preface vii
1 Our Orders Are Clear 11
2 Obey God First 18
3 We Have Dual Citizenship 24
4 Authorities: Created by God; Responsible to God 31
5 The Targets of Satan's Attacks 45
6 We Should Expect Suffering 59
7 Our Upside-Down World 66
8 A Closer Look at Spiritual Warfare 86
9 Action Triggers Miracles 99
10 The Truth, the Whole Truth .112
11 Should We Smuggle Bibles? .128
12 Can We Stand by and Do Nothing? 137
Epilogue 152
Notes 158

Acknowledgments

This book is an amplification of some of the ideas contained in a much earlier book of mine, *The Ethics of Smuggling*. It represents years of reflection and ministry experience, both mine and that of the Open Doors with Brother Andrew team.

Since my book was first published, a number of other books have appeared on the theme of Christians obeying or disobeying governments in order to worship and witness according to God's will.

I have carefully examined all such books that have come to my attention and am encouraged to see the tide is turning toward a more radical Christian commitment to carrying out the Great Commission. But for the reader who has encountered this issue for the first time, I have listed some of these books at the end of *Is Life So Dear?* I encourage you to read more on this subject. While I do not agree in all particulars with what these others have written, they are seeking an honest, biblical solution to the dilemma of obeying both God and governments.

I also wish to express my appreciation to many authors who have taken the time to discuss this subject with me. Their help and encouragement are reflected in these pages.

On the Open Doors team, I have been particularly helped by Dr. Dale W. Kietzman who supervised the drafting of this book. Special thanks, too, to Ruth Larssen who faithfully typed each draft and watched for flaws in my imperfect use of the English language. Many of the team joined in discussions on the ethical question involved in these chapters, and I am grateful for their help and support as well.

Preface

I dedicate this book to those Christians who throughout history have wound up on the wrong side of the law. Literally untold thousands of Christians have been arrested, imprisoned, tortured, deprived of possessions, or executed for their witness. The vast majority of them were not being punished for having done something against God—for having broken His law. Most had only broken the law of some human government.

The fact is, Christians can in all righteousness break certain laws. Otherwise, how did so many of our heroes of the faith wind up in prison? The list of martyrs beginning with Hebrews 11 has an appendix to it that extends through all the apostles; many of the church fathers; great men like William Tyndale, who made the Bible available to us; and John Bunyan, who gave us the powerful and deeply spiritual work, *Pilgrim's Progress*. It extends through missionary pioneers like Adoniram Judson, and modern leaders, such as Georgi Vins and Watchman Nee; as well as through countless unknown men and women whose only crime was that they chose for God. They were condemned by the action of the constituted authorities because they broke the law.

But the important aspect of their lives was not the laws they broke, but that they were a part of that select company who overcame Satan because "they did not hold their lives too dear to lay them down" (Rev. 12:11 NEB).

When God's Word tells us to "remember those who are in prison, as though in prison with them" (Heb. 13:3), God is saying that we should identify with those who have broken the laws of their countries.

Why were there believers in prison at the time the New Testament was being written? And why have Christians been imprisoned throughout the history of the church until this very day? Because these believers decided to obey God rather than man. They decided they would obey the laws of their countries only up to the point at which those laws transgressed the expressed will of God. Today, unfortunately, choices like this still must be made in many countries, especially those that are controlled by the doctrines of Marxism or Islam.

Persecution seems more intense and widespread than ever before. This increased persecution is an encouraging sign that the devil is mad at God's children. He's mad because the numbers of Christians are growing where there have been few Christians. But it remains discouraging that, in so-called Christian nations like the Netherlands or the United States or Great Britain, we fail to identify effectively with the suffering church; and church leaders in free countries even say about these brethren, "They've broken the law; therefore they should be punished."

But most Christians suffering today really are keeping *God's* law! And the church itself is now living in a time in which we may all have to break the law in order to continue to worship and obey God. In fact, we may have to break the law of man and of governments *in order* to keep the law of God.

I urge you to have enough backbone to agree with God. When the Word of God tells us to "remember those in bonds," or to identify with those who are in prison "as though in prison with them," it is giving us a principle by which the church in the end-time will not only survive, but also triumph. I believe that if we will accept God's will in this matter, we can become so strong that out of our midst—and I see this happening already—an army of young people will go into the world defying any man-made laws which try to shut out the gospel.

I was deeply moved when I first read the words of Patrick Henry, the American Revolutionary War hero, who said, "Is life so dear or peace so sweet as to be purchased at the price of chains and slavery?"

He was calling for political revolution. We call for a revolution of love. We need to know that spirit of uncompromising obedience that will say, "We hold not our lives dear unto death!"

Is life so dear or peace so sweet as to be purchased at the price of chains and slavery?
—Patrick Henry, March 23, 1775
(Speech before the Virginia convention)

By the sacrifice of the Lamb they have conquered him, and by the testimony which they uttered; for they did not hold their lives too dear to lay them down.
—Revelation 12:11 (NEB)

1
Our Orders Are Clear

Imagine that you are a soldier. Your commanding officer has ordered you to invade enemy-held territory, and you plan your attack to catch the opposition off guard by striking when and where he least expects it. But as you move forward, you discover that his fortifications are well-constructed. What's worse, he has somehow learned of your plan, because, suddenly, guns open fire and you are blasted into retreat.

When you report back to headquarters your commanding officer asks: "Well, did you capture that position?"

"No, sir," you reply. "The enemy won't let me."

Do you think you could get away with that answer? That isn't what warfare is all about. When a soldier receives an order, he is bound by his oath of allegiance to fight to the death to fulfill it. He won't let himself be stopped simply because the enemy is entrenched and armed to resist! He knows that before he starts on his mission. His commander knows it too. That obstruction must be overcome if the battle is to be won!

Exactly the same principle of allegiance and obedience applies to spiritual warfare where we may have to disobey civil authorities in order to obey the Lord's command. Yet a lot of Christian soldiers seem to be saying to their Commander, "We can't advance because the enemy disapproves of our objectives and is not willing to let us succeed."

Isn't that ridiculous! Of course the devil disapproves; that's what makes him an enemy. Of course he fights against the Lord's army; that's what an enemy does! Why then are so many Christians amazed, even immobilized, by the least sign of resistance to the gospel? Why are our feelings hurt when sinners scoff at our witness? Why do we adjust our schedules and programs for serving Christ to conform to the regulations and restrictions of the enemy?

I believe it is because we have forgotten who issued our orders that we are so prone to obey rules and manmade laws that forbid the preaching of the gospel.

The most basic principle for any Christian work is this: the Lord Jesus Christ, who crushed Satan and conquered death, commands us to invade this enemy-occupied world and reclaim it for God. We march under His *exclusive* authority. We make no deals with the foe. No compromises with evil authority. No concessions to godless governments. And no excuses to anybody.

What's more, the Lord has given His assurance that hell's own gates will not hold up against the ultimate advance of Christ's church. The devil's maneuvers and power-plays are just his last-ditch resistance to the overwhelming forces of the Righteous One.

And yet some Christian leaders advise retreat in the face of hostility. If they still recognize the weapon of faith, they have already placed it among their antiques!

Maybe our preaching has been at fault. The claims of the kingdom of God ought to come first in our preaching, but we have deviated from them. We have overemphasized salvation in our evangelistic services and have neglected to present the claims of Christ as Lord. Thus, we have weak converts. We've made the forgiveness of sins and a clean heart the only issues. They are not! A far more basic issue is the total claim of Christ upon the individual.

Jesus is King! That's the starting point for conversion, and that's the starting point for Christian service—as the enemies of the gospel have known from New Testament days until now. Unfortunately, many of God's children lack that conviction.

Why is this message of the kingdom of God so hated by every kind of humanism today? Why are there so few hymns on Christian warfare, or on the Second Coming in those Christian songbooks allowed to be published in the Soviet Union? Why, in East Germany, in order to reprint a hymnbook, were all the songs such as "The Lamb Upon the Throne" and "Onward, Christian Soldiers" removed? Because they talk about spiritual conflict, and that is what the authorities are afraid of! But we must stand clearly on the side of our King. When this glorious King commands us, it is not for us to question, argue, or hesitate; we should act.

Now, what are His orders to us?

All authority in heaven and on earth has been given to me. Go therefore and make disciples of all nations, baptizing them in the name of the Father and of the Son and of the Holy Spirit, teaching them to observe all that I have commanded you; and lo, I am with you always, to the close of the age (Matt. 28:18-20).

During those three years of training Jesus gave His disciples, He struggled greatly to make them understand that the love of God for people was not confined to the Jewish nation but indeed was for the whole world. He had to break through their sectarian pride to make them think bigger than their own nation or their own religion.

So, just days after He had died on the cross, Jesus faced the disciples. It was the day of His ascension, the day on which He was going to take His rightful place on the throne of God. He had something astounding to say to them, the most important statement ever made in this world. He was going to send them into enemy territory!

He knew, as no one else could, that the devil, the prince of this world, would do everything he could to stop believers from spreading the gospel of Christ—because that message would reclaim men from the kingdom of darkness to the kingdom of light.

Thus, Jesus sounded a battle cry. He made the breathtaking statement: "All authority in heaven and on earth has been given to me."

Can you sense the impact of His words? This had never been said before! He was telling His little group of followers that they were to go, under His absolute, divine authority, into all the world to make disciples among all nations. This was not the wishful thinking of a dreamer. This was the explicit command of the all-knowing and all-powerful Son of God! He wasn't asking them, He was telling them!

Now everyone can agree with the first part of Jesus' statement that He indeed has all authority *in heaven*. We don't dispute that, and that is probably why we want to go to heaven. No war, no revolution, no sin, no sickness, no hatred. God is there; there is love, joy, peace, and righteousness—the kingdom of God. But possibly we overemphasize the attraction of heaven and avoid the conflict of living as Christians *in this world*.

That is exactly why Karl Marx, who came from a Jewish-Christian home (his family converted to Protestantism when he was eight years old), wrote his terrible indictment of Christianity: "Religion...is the opiate of the people." Marx saw Christians avoiding Christ's commands and the obligations attached to them. For it is not just authority in heaven that is involved here, it is also "all authority on earth."

By the assertion of authority, Jesus defined the battlefield for us and set the goals of spiritual conflict. He has sent His followers into enemy territory to claim people who are held in

14

sin by Satan, behind whatever barrier—whether it be cultural, linguistic, or even governmental.

Realizing that it was Jesus who had sent them into enemy territory, the early church knew they did not need permission from someone else. They were not facing a human enemy. Rather, they were facing hostile ideas, religions, and political philosophies governing whole nations—indeed, which today govern whole continents. But in confronting such an enemy, they did not need permission; they had only to obey their Commander!

I have a good friend in one of the Communist countries. He is a real scholar, but doesn't work in his own profession—he works full-time for the Lord as an evangelist. He said to me once: "Andrew, people who always ask permission whenever they think they need it—whether from the government, or a city council, or the police if they want to give out tracts, or have a campaign or an open-air meeting, or anything like that—indicate their basic unwillingness to get on with the job!

"If they were simply obedient and wanted to do it, they would do it because Jesus told them to. People may not like it, or governments might disagree. But faithful Christians do get arrested; they do get into trouble; however, they can always explain, and they can always still apologize. *But they must first do the Lord's work.*"

I think he has a great truth there. We must act! And if we are arrested, we must remember that interrogation is an excellent way of communicating new ideas! A Christian can clearly present the claims of Christ in his responses. But we have to face the fact that the governments of this world simply are not for Christ.

When Jesus ordered His disciples to move out with the gospel into all the world, there were at least as many "curtains" obstructing their way as there are today. Maybe they were not made of bamboo or iron, but there were religious, political, and geographical curtains. Yet the disciples took the Word of God to people in bondage everywhere. Against deadly opposition, they invaded every corner of the Roman Empire, and beyond.

The major threat in the world today is communism, politically speaking. Its tremendous strength is this: there are no spectators. In communism everyone must be involved. Every Communist is a revolutionary.

Christianity today does not come close to that kind of participation. In our church life, 99 percent of the people are spectators. The only contribution they make is a small one in the collection plate. If we Christians are going to win the world, this situation must change drastically.

Our lack of insight into Satan's tactics concerns me very much. We must realize very clearly that we are involved in a spiritual battle, and reconciliation with the enemy is not possible. He can only be conquered by our obedience to the command of Jesus to go into all the world.

I have stood in the main squares of many Communist cities as thousands of people paraded by. I have watched them in Moscow, in Havana, in Bucharest, in Budapest, in Prague, in East Berlin, and in Peking. I have watched as the faithful carried the red banner; I have heard their revolutionary songs; I have seen the determination on their faces. I know they intend to conquer the world!

In most of those cities I was very much alone, but as I stood there, I had that precious little Book pressed close to my heart. It spoke to me and said: "At the name of Jesus every knee should bow, in heaven and on earth and under the earth, and every tongue confess that Jesus Christ is Lord, to the glory of God the Father" (Phil. 2:10–11). It made me feel so good to know that Jesus and I were the majority. There

16

was no need for me to be afraid. All I had to do was obey His orders.

The apostle Peter found this out very quickly, as we see in Acts 5. Right there in the beginning of the church's life and public ministry, the Jewish authorities disagreed with its message and its methods—and with its leaders. So the legal government, the one to which the Bible says you must submit, arrested the apostles.

In Acts 5:28, the high priest said, "We strictly charged you not to teach in this name, yet here you have filled Jerusalem with your teaching and you intend to bring this man's blood upon us."

Look closely at the reply Peter gave for himself and the apostles: "We must obey God rather than men" (Acts 5:29).

That's it. Here again is the main issue: Jesus said we must take the gospel into every country. If any of those countries resist—whether through the police, the government, the army, the culture, or even the religion—we still have the commission to go, regardless!

Since our conflict is spiritual, we can only find the answer to what we should do in the Bible. It tells us what our attitudes ought to be toward governments, including our own. Can we criticize our own governments in areas where we feel they go against God? Can we criticize other governments that are godless, cruel, and persecuting the church? Is there not some action we can take if we know there are Christians in a country who are faithful, but who are persecuted because they want to live under Christ's dominion? Or is there no way we can help?

Really, all issues boil down to just one: who is the rightful ruler of this world? If we answer this question first, then it will be obvious that many problems—such as questions about the ethics of Bible-smuggling—are not, in fact, core issues. They have been answered for us in the fact of Christ's lordship.

2
Obey God First

I have to admit that I have never been completely happy with the stigma of being called a smuggler. As most people do, I associate bad things with smuggling, such as narcotics, or the slave trade. There is implied the negative idea of breaking the law for illicit gain. But the name has stuck; and so I am stuck with it, although it has caused some unfounded notions about what "Bible smugglers" do and why we do it.

We are not some kind of spiritual stunt-men who go careening recklessly around the world, our little station wagons full of Bibles, trying to see how much we can get away with and not get caught. The plight of our persecuted brethren is far too desperate for us to pull tricks just for the fun of showing off. Our main purpose is not even Bible distribution; it is to minister to our brothers and sisters in Christ in the suffering church in the areas where they have their greatest need.

Actually, labels make little difference. If indeed we are smugglers, then we do God's work among God's people with God's supplies and according to God's orders. What matters is that we obey the Lord. We do what we do because we believe with all our hearts that it is right before God. No Christian should serve Christ on any other basis.

We do what we have been commanded to do by our sovereign Lord, whether we are permitted to do it in the open, or are forced to do it secretly. We are, in reality, special agents of a government not of this world!

I did not pick the title for my first book; others decided it for me. So, willy-nilly, I became "God's smuggler." I knew then that my personal security would be compromised, and therefore my lifelong ministry changed by that label; so I never allowed *God's Smuggler* to be published in Dutch, the language of my homeland. But the book became a best-seller throughout the world (it has appeared in over twenty languages), and I could no longer do some of the things I told about in the book. Still, I strongly believe that dedicated Christians can and should spread the Word by whatever means necessary. Now I go around the world preaching exactly that message.

The reaction of Christians to the idea of Bible-smuggling varies. Some pick up the basic concept of helping fellow members of the body of Christ and do exactly what I and my fellow couriers have done in their own way. Often these volunteer "smugglers" are tourists or businessmen, clergy or diplomats. They do what we did: discover the need, pray for guidance, order Bibles, and set off trusting God for two kinds of miracles:

- A miracle at the border so that the Word can get to its destination.
- A miracle so that they can find the right contact to whom they can hand the Bibles without danger.

These second-wave couriers—businessmen, diplomats, and others, all amateurs at the business—have gone from Japan to China, from Mexico and Spain to Cuba, from America and England to Moscow, and from Norway to Murmansk. They all recount experiences similar to mine: the need is tremendous, but God answers prayer and helps them to do the job.

Other Christians flatly reject the possibility of spreading the Word this way. When *Eternity* magazine carried several articles debating the subject of Bible-smuggling in their July, 1975, issue, one reader emphatically wrote: "If God wishes the people behind the Iron Curtain to receive His Word, He will see to it through the normal accepted channels."

When I read that, I was reminded of what one church leader said when William Carey wanted to spread the gospel in 1792: "Young man, sit down. When God pleases to convert the heathen, He will do it without your aid or mine."

Let me just say I really find it difficult to respond to people who argue, "You shouldn't smuggle. Breaking the law is sin. If it's God's will that the Russians or the Chinese get His Word, then He will provide it directly." For those people I have no message because they don't know church history, missionary history, the work of Bible translators—such as John Wycliffe and William Tyndale—or the work of the Bible societies. And to put it even stronger, they don't know the holy Scriptures.

The greatest contribution you or I can make to the world today is to lead it back to the authority of the Word of God. We can do that effectively only if we are people of one Book— people who believe that Book, study that Book, act upon the truths of that Book, and who pass on that Book.

I have traveled all over the world and been in all of the countries where political systems restrict the liberty of the church. I have also been in many countries, including some in the West, where such restrictions are not present, but where people are filled with fear over trends in their society. They ask me, "Brother Andrew, which way are we going?" They are afraid nothing can stop the progress of evil.

I disagree.

No nation that has kept the Word of God central to its way of life has fallen to godless revolution. And no individual Christian can be destroyed by the devil while the Word of God is central to his life.

I commend the Bible to you. If your faith is built on this firm foundation, you will not be shaken. If you know the truth of the Word of God, no one will ever turn you away from Jesus. All you need is the Book of God. John Wesley had the Book of God and had the liberty to teach the message of the Book. His preaching led politicians, industrialists, and others to action, and God saved Britain from a bloody revolution like the one that engulfed France. We can only be saved from a similar anarchy if we return to the Word of God.

John Wesley cried: "Give me the Book of God at any price!" That is precisely why we are taking Bibles to places where they are most needed. Still, a majority of Christians balk at the idea of doing what is necessary to accomplish this.

Approaching the problem on a strictly human level provides them with no answers. Author James L. Johnson's editorial, "To Smuggle or Not to Smuggle?", in the *Christian Bookseller* gives a good illustration of this struggle:

> Recently I gave a lecture on some of the great books produced in the last three years on Christian themes, among which was *God's Smuggler* by Brother Andrew. Afterwards, a young man of 19 or so asked me bluntly if smuggling wasn't after all breaking the law, and even if it was Bibles wasn't a Christian to give no offense in these matters?
>
> First, I tried to shape up the concept that smuggling Bibles through a Russian frontier was not the same as smuggling heroin, diamonds, or Democracy. However, that was a very weak point, because to the other side, Bibles were contraband—maybe worse in their eyes than anything else.
>
> Second, I pursued the idea that "those guys" were evil, and we, the church, including Brother Andrew, were good and straight, so this in itself ought to form some basis for smuggling in some of that good. And I felt I had a pretty good argument on that point, too, but I had to conclude, which I knew he would, that "goodness" is always in terms of who is looking from which direction.
>
> Finally, when we confronted each other again, I had only one

argument left: Acts 5:29. When [sic] the people got after Peter and his friends saying, "Did we not tell you that you should not teach in this name?"

To which Peter said, "We ought to obey God rather than man."

Well, I could tell by the look in his eyes that I had not fully satisfied his inquiry. I kind of knew it too. And yet I had come close to the whole issue without perhaps really realizing it.

For, ultimately, I concluded to him, Christianity is a revolutionary force. It emerged with Christ as a revolutionary who was crucified for "stirring up the people against Rome." And ever since, the Church's role in history has been to disseminate the Gospel, even at the expense of the dictates or restraints of men....

My answer may not fully satisfy even when the real issue is raised. But history proves that the "profile in courage" is never associated with a man debating the morality of an action designed to the fullest good of a fellow human being....[1]

The letters I receive now are no longer just questions about smuggling, but rather indicate the search for a new inner attitude to life. The complicated times in which we live, the far-reaching corruption in all layers of society, and the humanism that has penetrated church and theology often give them a sense of emptiness.

Our dilemma is in essence a search for leadership. It's interesting to see how thoroughly divided Christian leadership is on questions involving our stand for our Lord, particularly when that requires doing something governments do not sanction. When the *Evangelical Newsletter* took a poll on the subject of civil disobedience in 1982, the range of responses was confusing at best: fifteen for, sixteen against, and thirty-three indicating major reservations of one kind or another. Some would tolerate civil disobedience only if related to specific causes: nuclear weapons, racism, abortion.

When we receive uncertain directions from Christian leaders, we should expect uncertain results.

In this bewildering leadership vacuum, another authority structure with another message presents itself: the cause of revolution proclaimed by a totalitarian regime with an absolute claim on the whole person—body, soul, and spirit—under the label of liberation.

Individuals who find it hard to accept the possibility that Christians might have to break the law are no match for these overwhelming forces. Such individuals do not have an answer to the questions we have raised up till now, nor do they have a defense against brute force. They are part of that great majority who remain silent in the face of naked evil: crime, hate, pornography, revolution, and corruption.

During a campaign in Johannesburg, South Africa, a man rushed up and handed me a letter. I just had time before the message to open it and read this: "Paul, writing to the Romans, says governments are put in authority by God for the maintenance of law and order."

Then there were three questions:

- Is the Communist government put in authority by God?
- Were other totalitarian governments, for example Hitler's and the Roman Empire's, placed by God?
- Can a Christian criticize his government when it goes against the Word of God?

I was startled. I had planned to speak on the Great Commission. Suddenly I realized that this whole issue of Bible-smuggling, which some people regard as a legal issue, can be restated simply as the age-old question: Should we obey man rather than God? Should we evangelize the whole world, as Christ told us to do, or stop short on the order of a hostile government?

3
We Have Dual Citizenship

Dual citizenship is an interesting concept, a remarkable legal phenomenon. Consider its implications.

Almost anyone born of parents who are outside of their own country at the time of birth have dual citizenship. Many sons and daughters of missionaries have dual citizenship: they are citizens of the country in which they were born and also of the country in which their parents are citizens. And if mother and father are citizens of two different countries, depending upon specific laws, the child might even have a claim to citizenship in three different countries!

Dual citizenship gives some unique advantages and can also, I imagine, cause great confusion at times. But it definitely gives a person rights in both countries, and this has a spiritual application.

The apostle Paul had dual citizenship by birth. His parents were Jewish—that gave him rights and obligations in the Jewish nation, including special privileges accorded him by Rome—and he was born in the Roman city of Tarsus, which gave him citizenship as a Roman. He often used both citizenships to his advantage in his travels.

A person with dual citizenship can identify with either country. He may even do this alternately, if he so desires and has not taken steps that irrevocably commit him to one or the other citizenship. Such a commitment might involve service in the military of one country that may terminate rights of citizenship in the other country.

Now these choices that have to be made by dual citizens suggest some of the struggles we go through as Christians. We are all, in effect, citizens of both the kingdom of God and of some earthly nation. Peter says that, as believers, we belong to "a chosen race, a royal priesthood, a holy nation, God's own people" (1 Pet. 2:9). Isn't it tremendous that when we are born again we are born with all the rights of a citizen in God's kingdom!

But Peter takes this analogy a step further, because he immediately tells us where our primary loyalty ought to be. In verse 11 of First Peter 2, he calls us "aliens and exiles" in this world. You see, our heavenly citizenship immediately takes precedence, demands our loyalties, and precludes dependence upon earthly rights, because as "aliens and exiles" we have no rights!

This description of our position in this world echoes the phrase contained in the honor roll of heroes of the faith in Hebrews 11: "These all died in faith...having acknowledged that they were strangers and exiles on the earth" (v. 13). This was the basis for their suffering as an example for us.

The apostles were also confronted with the question of whether or not they should submit to the earthly authorities—or whether they should accept the obligations of their heavenly calling. Peter and John were brought before the Sanhedrin (the duly established religious authority for the Jewish nation), arrested for ministering in the name of Jesus, and forbidden to "speak or teach at all in the name of Jesus" (Acts 4:18). To this, the apostles replied: "Whether it is right in the sight of God to listen to you rather than to God, you must judge; for we cannot but speak of what we have seen and heard" (Acts 4:19-20).

The apostles persisted in their activities. Once again they

were brought before the Sanhedrin and given strict orders to cease teaching in Jesus' name. Their response: "We must obey God rather than men" (Acts 5:29). How then, can we account for this defiance of authority? The key lies in the priority of allegiance. God was first, the government second. When commands of an established earthly authority conflict with divine commands, the Christian is obligated to follow the commands of God.

Corrie ten Boom, a fellow "smuggler" from Holland, told in the foreword she wrote to an earlier book of mine about the efforts of her family to save Jews during World War II. Her family came to a moment of decision when they learned that all the babies in a Jewish orphanage in Amsterdam were to be killed. She wrote, "Though I knew it was against the law of that time to interfere, I also knew we had to do something for those little ones."[1]

So she talked to the young people who were working with the ten Booms, and together they came up with a plan to save the babies. That same day, the boys in their group "stole" the babies. The girls took them and knocked on many doors where many arms opened to receive those frightened little bundles of humanity. We all recognize that the Christians in Hitler-held Europe were justified in resisting the atrocities of the Nazis by providing aid and comfort to the Jewish people when and wherever possible.

The ten Boom family continued to hide Jews in their home up over the watchmaker's shop until they all were arrested. Many of the family died during those tragic days, but they "obeyed God rather than men."

The accounts of acts of self-sacrifice by committed Christians during the bloody years of the Hitler era could be greatly expanded. From preachers to bakers, from military officers to gardeners, rich and poor, high and low, young and old—many responded to the proddings of God's Spirit to act against the government.

We Have Dual Citizenship

Scripture abounds in examples of times when loyalty to God was primary. Hebrew midwives spared the lives of the male children in violation of the edict of Egypt's king (Ex. 1:15–20). The mother of Moses hid her child contrary to Pharaoh's order (Ex. 2:2-3). Daniel disobeyed the royal decree by courageously continuing to kneel in prayer—before an open window—three times daily (Dan. 6). The question was not, is it legal? But rather, who has the right to declare that obeying God is illegal?

As Paul preached to unbelievers, he didn't just talk about the sin in their hearts. Although that was part of his message, he spoke primarily about the kingdom of God. He told them there was another country, and by believing on the Lord Jesus Christ they could become citizens of that country. Paul said in Philippians 3:20: "But our commonwealth is in heaven, and from it we await a Savior, the Lord Jesus Christ." Now the Greek word Paul used for commonwealth really means political habitation—another country with another set of laws, another constitution because there is another King.

As Paul preached to unbelievers, he was in effect saying that there is no compromise possible between these two systems. You cannot cross over a heathen bridge into the kingdom of God. There is only one bridge between your philosophy and the kingdom of God. That is the cross of Jesus Christ.

Paul said "to Jews, it is foolishness; and to others, a stumbling block." But no compromise is possible. Jesus Christ is crucified, and only by accepting that, can you enter the kingdom of God. Thus Jesus does not merely become your savior, but also your King! You've got to break with all other allegiances; place your life totally under the rule of Jesus Christ, the King, Paul would say.

In every moral and ethical question that we face today, we must acknowledge there is a higher authority and a primary citizenship responsibility involved. We have placed our lives under God's authority as Scripture indicates. In Acts 5:29 the authorities tell Peter that he cannot preach and teach anymore in the name of Jesus. Do you think Peter replied, "Yes, I happen to be a citizen of this country so I submit myself to you and your rules"? If he had done so, how many of us would be Christians today?

Peter said, "No, I have a higher allegiance; I must obey God rather than men."

Of course, not every law of man conflicts with God's law, but some laws do. Nurses or doctors, for instance, have to face what they will do about abortion, a widely accepted practice today, because God's law is a law of life. Which allegiance will we honor?

In Acts 19, the apostle Paul upset authorities in Ephesus. Paul and his companions had seen remarkable results in that city. Secular history tells us there may have been as many as twenty thousand believers in the city of Ephesus after only three years of preaching there. You can readily understand the terrible uproar.

Have you ever noticed that the devil often uses the masses? Only God dares to work through a single individual, because one man with God is a majority.

Listen to the town clerk as he speaks to that crowd in Ephesus: "You have brought these men here who are neither sacrilegious nor blasphemers of our goddess" (Acts 19:37). Paul had been there more than two years and in those years he had not directly spoken against their goddess, Diana.

When the implications of what the town clerk of Ephesus had said got through to me, it was quite a revelation! Paul's success was not based on the matters he "took a stand against." Paul achieved success by what he stood for: he was for Jesus; he was for the kingdom of God. That is why God blessed his ministry.

Many Christians today need to discover that we do not have

to be negative. The church of Christ can survive under any political or economic system. Don't think that communism is the biggest enemy of Christianity, or that Islam is an impregnable force opposed to Christianity. It may well be that the luxuries of capitalism have killed more spiritual Christians than communism has. But I am not going to spend my time fighting capitalism either because I live in another kingdom. I live under other rules and laws. My king is Jesus.

I think the fact of the Christian's dual citizenship and his need to be committed to the kingdom of God is very clear in the Scriptures. But we have compromised so badly with the world's systems, even though the Bible tells us not to do so, that we hardly notice the point at which any given government disobeys God.

Jesus made an interesting response in Matthew 22:20-21 to people who had a tricky question for Him about paying taxes. When they showed Him a coin He asked: " 'Whose likeness and inscription is this?' They said, 'Caesar's.' Then He said to them, 'Render therefore to Caesar the things that are Caesar's, and to God the things that are God's.' When they heard it, they marveled; and they left Him and went away"—unable to make up their minds and unwilling to make a choice.

What did Jesus say here? The coin indeed had the image of Caesar imprinted on it. So, in this and other aspects of life, if it has Caesar's imprint, give it to Caesar. But if it has God's imprint, give it to God.

When Jesus looked at the people, He saw people made in the *likeness* of God! He was clearly saying: give *that* to God, *give yourself* to God! And I tell you that if you give yourself to God—wholly, completely—there is very little left for Caesar. That is what Jesus says to us.

Our problem is that there are millions of Christians who cannot make up their minds—who want to live in a no-man's-land. They want something for everybody: a little bit of the left and a little bit of the right. But they never take a clear stand for Jesus Christ.

Romans 12:1 makes it clear what God wants from us: "I appeal to you, therefore, brethren, by the mercies of God, to present your bodies as a living sacrifice, holy and acceptable to God, which is your spiritual worship."

Then Paul adds, "Do not be conformed to this world." Don't bother about it. Don't get involved in it. Work for the kingdom of God. Be a radical, or even a fanatic for it! Someone once said it's easier to cool down a fanatic than to warm up a corpse any day! Jesus said, "So, because you are lukewarm, and neither cold nor hot, I will spew you out of my mouth" (Rev. 3:16).

If we were all out for Jesus Christ, then we would obey God, and we would also discover ourselves in compliance with all the human laws that are in harmony with God's will.

We know what God's will is; we just try to dodge His commandments. That gets us into all kinds of trouble. As William Penn said in 1681: "If we are not governed by God, then we will be ruled by tyrants."

4
Authorities: Created by God; Responsible to God

Many people have said to me, "You are breaking the law. If the law in a country says no Bibles are permitted, you should not bring them in."

These people would be absolutely right if we did not recognize the law of the Lord as well as the law of a particular country. These two laws are often in direct opposition to each other. But God's law always has priority.

When Jesus was asked to identify the greatest commandment, He quoted verses which every Jewish child knew from Deuteronomy 6:4–7:

> The LORD our God is one LORD; and you shall love the LORD your God with all your heart, and with all your soul, and with all your might. And these words which I command you this day shall be upon your heart; and you shall teach them diligently to your children, and shall talk of them when you sit in your house, and when you walk by the way, and when you lie down, and when you rise.

"You shall teach them...to your children." That's God's law. Jesus reflected its spirit when He said: "Let little children come to me." Now the law of godless regimes says you cannot teach children about Jesus; you cannot teach them to pray; you cannot teach them the Bible, or take them to church. It's forbidden.

Let there be no doubt: if we are consistent in keeping the law of God, of necessity we will have to break some of the laws of civil governments. When countries with godless, atheistic governments tell us not to teach children about Jesus or not to take Bibles in, we've *got* to break their law or break God's.

We are to reach *all* nations with the gospel, making disciples of *all* nations, including Russia, Mongolia, China, Tibet (you can name all of the Communist countries, right-wing dictatorships, Islamic regimes, whatever). If we write off any of them because we say they are behind borders that are unpleasant to us, we establish a tradition that we want to be nice to the devil! We even want to lend him a hand as he kills God's children and tries to prevent the coming of the kingdom of God! In doing that, we definitely break the law of God!

Jesus did not send us only to countries that would welcome us, yet we tend to send missionaries only to countries that put out the red carpet. We think of "open doors" only in terms of a welcome to Christian workers, but, are there ever any "closed" doors for our King?

That question brings us squarely to the controversy over methods. I do not believe our Lord is willing for His Word and witness to be kept out of any country by guarded boundaries or government decrees.

Take the example of Christian radio. I heartily support the work of Christian radio stations that beam the gospel into Communist countries. Most Christians endorse such broadcasts. But the Russian government is just as much against gospel broadcasts as they are against literature carried over the border. It's all the same to them. Both meet the same resistance on their side and both originate from the same commission on our side.

Yet we must confront this sensitive issue of obeying governments on all possible levels and not just encourage disobedience. We must obey the government (whether it is our own, or the government of a nation where God sends us) *unless that government takes the place of God*. A government can attempt to take the place of God when it tries to restrict true worship or limits the possibility of a believer's witness to his faith.

Of course, since all authority is from God, and His revelation establishes valid ethical standards, there should be no conflict in principle between the church and the state, if each carries out its proper role. God does not give to either one the rights or responsibilities of the other. If God commands us to worship Him freely and to preach His Word widely, no civil government should try to prevent us from doing that.

Governments are as much subject to the moral judgment and direction of God as are individuals. Unfortunately, governments often violate God's moral standards. Thus, if a government passes a law preventing the distribution of the Word of God, that legislation is unlawful in the sight of God. The state has transgressed its God-ordained boundaries, and the Christian does not have to obey such a law.

The requirement of our subjection to government is always qualified. We are subject only to the state's lawful commands and must not obey when the state violates the laws of God. Absolute obedience belongs only to God.

At this point, some might quote that venerable theologian, John Calvin, who argued we are obligated to obey even unjust magistrates and evil kings. In one section of his *Institutes* he said we must "be very careful not to despise or violate that authority of magistrates...even though it may reside with the most unworthy men." But in another section entitled "Obedience to Man Must not Become Disobedience to God," he said:

> But in that obedience which we have shown to be due the authority of rulers, we are always to make the exception, indeed, to observe it as primary, that such obedience is never to lead us away from obedience to Him, to whose will the desires of all kings ought to be subject, to whose decrees all their commands ought to yield, to whose majesty their scepters ought to be submitted. And how absurd would it be that in satisfying men you should incur the displeasure of Him for whose sake you obey men themselves! The Lord, therefore, is the King of Kings, who, when He has opened His sacred mouth, must alone be heard, before all and above all men; next to Him we are subject to those men who are in authority over us, but only in Him. If they command anything against Him, let it go unesteemed.[1]

From Calvin, we go to the apostle Paul's discussion of this whole matter in Romans 13. His words especially interest me because I lived through five years of German occupation in the Netherlands. On the basis of Romans 13, some fine believers cooperated with the German occupation army, considering it to be the legal government. They felt justified in cooperating because Paul said there was no power or authority but that which is instituted by God. Others, equally pious, refused to cooperate, and, in fact, actively resisted.

Paul states in Romans 13: 1-6:

> Let every person be subject to the governing authorities. For there is no authority except from God, and those that exist have been instituted by God. Therefore he who resists the authorities resists what God has appointed, and those who resist will incur judgment. For rulers are not a terror to good conduct, but to bad. Would you have no fear of him who is in authority?

Then do what is good, and you will receive his approval, for he is God's servant for your good. But if you do wrong, be afraid, for he does not bear the sword in vain; he is the servant of God to execute his wrath on the wrongdoer. Therefore one must be subject, not only to avoid God's wrath, but also for the sake of conscience. For the same reason you also pay taxes, for the authorities are ministers of God, attending to this very thing.

Paul says there is no authority except from God, but he does define the kind of authority and government he has in mind. Proper government protects the good, and he who does good will receive its approval. Sound governmental rulers are God's servants for the people's good.

Is that really the case with godless authorities?

Paul made another statement about civil authorities in 1 Timothy 2:1–4:

First of all, then, I urge that supplications, prayers, intercessions, and thanksgivings be made for all men, for kings and all who are in high positions, that we may lead a quiet and peaceable life, godly and respectful in every way. This is good, and it is acceptable in the sight of God our Savior, who desires all men to be saved and to come to the knowledge of the truth.

Again, Paul defines the task of good government. It is to insure that we have religious liberty so we can fulfill the laws of Christ, and His law desires that all men be saved and come to the knowledge of the truth! Paul links this idea to our prayers for an attitude toward a legal government.

When a government, local, national, or international, limits the church in its activity and curbs the witness of Christians, or perhaps persecutes them, it has gone beyond the purposes of the God who ordained it. Thus, we are no longer under obligation to observe its regulations with respect to witness and worship. We are free because God has defined the role of government. We must obey and glorify Christ with a pure conscience. To obey a government that oppresses the church would be just as misguided as when some Dutch people obeyed the German occupation—or as it would have been for Jews to obey Hitler.

I am so glad the Bible makes this clear. In the *New English Bible,* 1 Timothy 2:2 reads: "...that we may lead a tranquil and quiet life in full observance of religion." Full observance means to go into all the world in obedience to our Lord's command. Whenever any government restricts the traveling of Christians to witness, then we must go in spite of the government's regulation.

Let me support that with another Scripture, one written about the actions of the apostle whose instructions we are interpreting here. In Acts 9:23, Saul was in Damascus when the Jews plotted to kill him. This plan was not the action of an individual; it was from the government. The Jews had an official warrant of arrest probably similar to the one Saul had been given for his mission to persecute the church in Damascus. Saul was in trouble because, instead of persecuting the church, he was now witnessing for Jesus Christ after his wonderful encounter with the risen Lord.

We read, "But their plot became known to Saul. They were watching the gates day and night" (Acts 9:24). Who was watching? The government; police and soldiers (2 Cor. 11:32–33)! But his companions helped him get away at night by lowering him in a basket down over the wall.

Saul committed an illegal act by avoiding border controls and fleeing arrest. Shouldn't he have submitted to the government? Didn't it have the power of God?

No! Saul believed that to fully observe the commandments of Christ, he must not let the authorities control his activities. Inasmuch as he had already received the commandment to evangelize, he could not be bogged down by government decrees.

In fact, he didn't even accept punishment if it came his way unjustly. For Paul did not consider that the word he used of our relationship to government, *subjection,* required him to accept an immoral judgment from the state. If the command of a government was unlawful, then the penal sanction attached to it was unlawful. If one could resist the former, then he was equally justified in resisting the latter.

The apostle Paul frequently did not accept the established procedures and punishments prescribed by magistrates as is shown by Scripture (see Acts 17:6-10; 19:38-20:1). He simply disregarded some of the rules that people who are not in his business of preaching the gospel should observe. That is why Paul was so often in prison. It was not for doing legal things but always for doing illegal things.

Paul faced another dangerous situation in Iconium (Acts 14:6). The people there tried to arrest and stone him, but he and his companions learned of it and fled to Lystra and Derbe, where they continued to preach the gospel.

They fled!

"You shouldn't flee, Paul. You shouldn't run out. Why, you should submit to the government!"

To which Paul might have replied: "Not when they restrict me in my witness for Jesus Christ. Then I must go against them and do what Jesus told me and let no one interfere with me."

Another time, in Thessalonica, Paul had to hide because local citizens had attacked the house of Jason, seeking to bring him out so they could take him before the local government. The rioters couldn't find him because he had concealed his mission—he had gone "underground," in a way (Acts 17:5-6). He was not going to allow his work and witness to be destroyed by the enemy. He was not going to submit to what people would call the legal government.

In yet another situation, a mob tried to stir up the city of Ephesus. Paul had made many converts there and angered some local businessmen who profited from the worship of the pagan goddess, Diana. Naturally, he wanted to defend himself—and to witness—but his companions would not let him. They hid him and forced him to get out of the city. They took the blame for what Paul was supposed to have done (Acts 19: 30–31).

Here is a crucial point. Paul and his fellow believers recognized the real issue: they knew the government was against God, but they had a mission to carry out that must not be stopped. They were under higher authority than the government's.

At the end of a discussion begun in Romans 13 about the hazards of conduct in uncharted situations, Paul states: "The faith that you have, keep between yourself and God; happy is he who has no reason to judge himself for what he approves. But he who has doubts is condemned, if he eats, because he does not act from faith; for whatever does not proceed from faith is sin" (Rom. 14:22–23). That's why it is so important for each of us to know where we stand on this issue of authority and what Scripture has to say about it.

It is perfectly clear from Paul's life that his pride in his Roman citizenship (Acts 22:28) and his general loyalty to the laws of the empire never took the place of his unreserved obedience to the Lord Jesus Christ, even when it might mean death! He respected authority, but he knew which authority had the supreme claim on his allegiance.

Paul also knew that some Christians might make different judgments. He did not want to argue with them. In Galatians 6:17, he seems to give his final word on the subject: "Henceforth let no man trouble me; for I bear on my body the marks of Jesus." He simply was not going to spend more energy proving his points. You may not agree with what he did, but by his scars you knew he did it all for Jesus.

Not all of the New Testament teaching on governments comes from Paul. Peter's statements and experiences are also worth examining. In his first epistle we read:

> Be subject for the Lord's sake to every human institution, whether it be to the emperor as supreme, or to governors as sent by him to punish those who do wrong and to praise those who do right. For it is God's will that by doing right you should put to silence the ignorance of foolish men. Live as free men, yet without using your freedom as pretext for evil; but live as servants of God. Honor all men. Love the brotherhood. Fear God. Honor the emperor (1 Pet. 2:13–17).

He calls for authority to be honored, and God to be feared. He says the government must comply with this criterion: It must punish wrongdoers, and praise those who do right. When this does not happen, then the whole structure falls apart, and there is no reason to obey such a government.

All we need to do is look at Peter's life to see that he did not believe governments always need to be obeyed. One confrontation Peter had with the authorities is recorded in Acts 5:17. Here, the apostles were under pressure from a government they were to honor and obey—a government that was supposed to punish the bad and praise the good—but one that had put them in prison.

The Scripture says an angel from the Lord opened the prison doors. Highly illegal! You can't just open prison doors like that; they were closed and guarded by order of a government put there by God! Yet God identified with the men who defied the government. God Himself takes the apostles out of prison; and what's more, God doesn't say to them: "Now, disappear, go underground." No! He says, "Go and stand in the temple and speak to the people all the words of this Life" (Acts 5:20).

Doesn't that strike you as humorous, really? God is not afraid of a confrontation with the powers of evil; we are the ones who are afraid because we don't know the real issues. That's why, at least as I believe, what I do isn't smuggling at all: it's only obeying God rather than men!

In Peter's case, when the authorities catch up with the apostles again and warn them: " 'We strictly charged you not to teach in this name [an official government decree], yet here you have filled Jerusalem with your teaching and you intend to bring this man's blood upon us' " (Acts 5:28). He replies: " *'We must obey God rather than men.'* "

There is a choice, you see. You can obey man, and you can obey the government, sure! You need not do anything for Jesus in your whole lifetime—and let the whole world go to hell while the name of Christ is ridiculed.*

If we are going to cite the Bible as our authority, we must take verses in their context. Submission to civil, legal authorities is a principle that the Scriptures very clearly and carefully qualifies.

One important consideration is what constitutes a legal government. If an occupation army comes, is that our government? Or are the authorities in exile or underground our legal government?

The same question pertains specifically to the matter of dictatorships, whether of the right or of the left. None of the governments in Eastern Europe is there by the choice of the people. I dare say that 95 percent of the population hates their government in Eastern Europe and the Soviet Russia.

---

*I would particularly call your attention to the position of Francis Schaeffer in *A Christian Manifesto*, (Westchester, Ill.: Crossway Books, 1981), where he argues that at times Christians have a *duty to disobey* the state, pp. 93ff, 130.

Are these, then, legal governments? You could doubt that.

At any rate, such dictatorships surely are not ours. Nor can we recognize them as God-appointed governments inasmuch as those authorities act against the expressed will of God which says that the gospel shall be preached to everyone. Therefore, we must bypass them and carry out the Great Commission of Jesus Christ our Lord.

Perhaps John Calvin, the Reformation theologian much-honored in my own Dutch Calvinistic upbringing, can help us, because, he, too, wrestled with this problem of obedience to authority (for his full discussion, see his *Institutes of the Christian Religion*, Book Four, chapter XX, 23–32). He cites Romans 13:1–12, Titus 3:1, 1 Peter 2:13–14, and 1 Timothy 2:1–2 to indicate that obedience is also due unjust magistrates, and even suggests a wicked ruler might be a judgment from God. He cites many Old Testament references as a foundation for this belief, and for his assertion that obedience to bad kings is required in Scripture.

Calvin coupled his strong argument for obedience to authorities, whether just or unjust, to a belief that God would always provide defenders of a people's freedom. Since he himself was involved in political matters, he simply assumed that representative bodies or parliaments would moderate or punish the actions of unjust rulers.

But even Calvin had to make an exception to his firm stand on submission. He concluded that obedience to governments is never to lead us away from obedience to God. In the section, "Obedience to Man Must Not Become Disobedience to God" from the *Institutes,* he writes:

> But since this edict has been proclaimed by the heavenly herald, Peter—"We must obey God rather than men" [Acts 5:29]—let us comfort ourselves with the thought that we are

rendering that obedience which the Lord requires when we suffer anything rather than turn aside from piety. And that our courage may not grow faint, Paul pricks us with another goad: That we have been redeemed by Christ at so great a price as our redemption cost Him, so that we should not enslave ourselves to the wicked desires of men—much less be subject to their impiety [1 Cor. 7:23].[2]

Calvin might well have referred to one of the psalms which also makes the point so clearly: "For the wicked shall not rule the godly, lest the godly be forced to do wrong" (Ps. 125:3 TLB).

Here is an illustration of that truth from the Old Testament. In Daniel 3, King Nebuchadnezzar had set up a huge image and called together all his people, including many Jewish prisoners who were living in Babylon in exile, to hear this edict: "When you hear the sound of the horn, pipe, lyre, trigon, harp, bagpipe, and every kind of music, you are to fall down and worship the golden image that King Nebuchadnezzar has set up; and whoever does not fall down and worship shall immediately be cast into a burning fiery furnace" (vv. 5–6).

This rule comes from the government, the legal authority, acknowledged as such not just by Babylonians but also by the Jews who had submitted themselves to it, including a man of God like Daniel who eventually served as a minister in three successive governments and who must have acknowledged this as his legal government.

When Daniel's three friends heard this decree, and when the music was played and everybody fell down before the image and worshiped, they refused to bow and so were cast into the fiery furnace. (Daniel himself is absent from this story, perhaps absent from the city at the time.)

Although the government of Nebuchadnezzar tried to take the place of God, the king discovered an amazing limitation to his power. When he looked into the furnace, he saw four men, not just the three, walking free in the midst of the fire, unharmed; and the appearance of the fourth was like "the Son of God" (Dan. 3:25 KJV).

God Himself had identified with those who disobeyed the king's command. Because there was a more important issue at stake than mere acknowledgment of a ruler, those who refused to obey the ungodly decree were in the will of God and preserved by Him!

This demonic desire for equality with God manifests itself in two areas. First, in the area of worshiping the Lord. And second, in the fact that godless governments obstruct Christians from serving the Lord Jesus Christ and witnessing for Him.

When Christians are persecuted for their faith, it always has to do with these two aspects of the life of faith. Restrictions in these areas are something we cannot accept as God's will. If a people choose socialism, that is to a certain degree their own decision to make; if a government forbids the smuggling of tobacco or milk-powder, it has a right to do so. But if the authorities interfere with our conscience, preventing Christians from worshiping God and restricting Christian testimony, then we have to resist.

The issue was the same for Daniel, Peter, or Paul as it is for our time. What so many regard as an ethical issue, "Oh, you shouldn't smuggle Bibles; you should keep the law," is nothing more than an agreement with the devil. In spending our energies debating the morality of specific kinds of witnessing or worship, we deny God the right to rule the world. And that's exactly why the devil rules it.

We need to go back to Matthew 28:18–19 where Jesus first claims He has all authority, both in heaven and on earth. Only then does He command, "Go therefore..." He implies that we do not need anybody else's permission. We don't have to confer with our enemy and have a nice conference to discuss our plans. We simply have to go. We are going into enemy-occupied territory and only One has the rightful claim to the world: God, through Jesus Christ, His Son! He has redeemed men by His cross and has given His followers the commission to share this good news and appeal to people everywhere to be converted.

In New Testament days, political life depended on loyalty to Caesar. The cry of the day was "Caesar is Lord." But, as evangelist Billy Graham notes, for the new band of Christians, another loyalty was at the center of their lives: "Jesus is Lord," not Caesar. "In spite of the admonitions of Paul and Peter to worship God and honor the emperor, this act of Caesar-worship was impossible. And because of their refusal to put Caesar before Christ, Christian believers began to be persecuted," Dr. Graham observes.[3]

God's Word requires submissiveness of heart to all authority, but absolute obedience only to God. In practical terms, this explains why Paul, Peter, and other disciples obeyed "God rather than men" and cheerfully accepted the consequences of prison sentences and death. They sang in prison, not in noisy protest, but in happy submission to authority and its consequences—"counting it all joy" to suffer for Christ's sake (James 1:2).

5
The Targets of Satan's Attacks

Have you ever noticed the strategy Satan used throughout Old Testament history? His attacks were aimed at preventing the birth of the Messiah at Bethlehem, but, once Jesus was born, Satan's tactics changed somewhat. In some instances, he tried to kill Jesus before the Lord could reach the cross. At other times, Satan engineered numerous attempts to discredit Him—to cause Him to stumble or to sin.

But Satan met defeat at the cross. He failed to understand God's strategy, and his final blunder actually forced events so that Jesus, though innocent, was condemned to die. The apostle Paul noted that "none of the rulers of this age [headed by Satan] understood this; for if they had, they would not have crucified the Lord of glory" (1 Cor. 2:8).

Since that time, Satan's tactics have changed. He's still concerned about preventing the Word—the Word that was with God and is God (John 1:1)—from reaching people who are under Satan's dominion. His attack is now two-pronged.

First, Satan concentrates on the life and name of Jesus which each and every believer bears as the Lord's representative. I believe it is important for Christians undergoing persecution to realize the attack they are under is actually directed not at them, but at the life of Jesus in them, a life which they have the power to transmit to others.

Satan will make every effort to discredit you, to frighten

45

you, and to silence your witness in order that the new life in you stops with you. Sometimes Satan overreaches himself, just as he did at the cross, and sends a believer to a martyr's grave, but that life lives on in other believers who continue to bear witness more gloriously and triumphantly than ever. That the church not only survives, but grows under such persecution has been demonstrated beautifully by the church in China. After missionaries were expelled in 1950, and all ties were cut with the rest of the body of Christ, believers were put through the horrible experience of Mao's cultural revolution. Christians were killed or imprisoned, Bibles burned, and the remaining believers scattered all over China. The attack was clearly on the life and name of Jesus as manifested in believers' lives.

As these sufferers scattered, they took the life of Jesus with them, and just as was the case with the early believers in Jerusalem, "Those who were scattered went about preaching the Word" (Acts 8:4). Only now are we beginning to see the harvest in China, as millions of Christians are identified, meeting together for fellowship and worship in remote provinces.

The second prong of Satan's attack is on the written Word of God. He has historically tried to prevent Christians from having access to the Bible.

Satan understands the power of the Word of God. At the temptation of Jesus, he even made a sly attempt to use Scripture (actually misapplying it) to deflect Jesus from His true mission (Luke 4: 1–3). Twisting Scripture is still a favorite tactic of Satan, and we believers need to know the Word so we can respond, just as Jesus did, with a well-applied "It is written..."

Satan has spared no effort to keep the Bible well away from inquiring hearts and from believers who could be made more bold in their witness as they fed upon it. Thus the history of the church is punctuated with attempts to ban the Bible.

Peter recognized the significant role the Word has in our salvation. In his epistle to Christians soon to pass through a "fiery trial," he gives this word of encouragement: "You have been born anew, not of perishable seed but of imperishable, through the living and abiding word of God; for 'All flesh is like grass and all its glory like the flower of grass. The grass withers, and the flower falls, but the word of the Lord abides forever'" (1 Pet. 1:23-25).

Now you can understand my life's passion to distribute the Bible, even in places where its importation or distribution is prohibited. Because I go around the world preaching that message, many people assume that I must have been the first "God's smuggler." Nothing could be further from the truth.

I personally believe that the first Bible smuggler probably was Timothy, the man Paul looked upon as his son in the gospel. This young man of delicate health, but of great spirituality and loyalty, was converted in Paul's first campaign at Lystra.

At the end of his life, when Paul was in prison in Rome, he looked to Timothy for comfort. In a letter to him, Paul asked his friend to bring his books to the prison the next time he visited.

In 2 Timothy 4:13 it becomes clear Paul was requesting that scrolls of Old Testament Scriptures be brought to him for further study. But how could Timothy get them into Rome and into the jail when, by that time, Christians had already become an outlawed sect? The only possible way would have been to smuggle them in with other items.

Billy Graham suggests that John the apostle had to write his Revelation secretly, while closely guarded by the Romans. "Now the cave is empty, but his pile of rough parchment pages are stacked neatly in a secret hollow or beneath a straw sleeping mat. One day those pages will be smuggled off the island. One day Christian volunteers will copy down what John wrote and deliver the Revelation of Jesus Christ to the churches of Asia."[1]

There were many severe persecutions directed against Christians during the next two centuries, but the first attempt to burn or destroy all Scriptures then available in the Roman Empire came in A.D. 303, with an edict of the Emperor Diocletian. However, only a few years later, Christianity became a recognized religion under Constantine, and Bibles could once more be possessed openly.

Then, instead of using civil monarchs to repress the Bible, the devil very subtly used the church itself. Over the next several centuries, the principal agency limiting Bible distribution was the church. Only Latin Scriptures were available, and then, only to the clergy. For all practical purposes, the Bible was entombed in a dead language and hidden inside monasteries through all the Dark Ages. By 1229, the church had reached the point of prohibiting laymen from possessing Scripture, and in 1234, a law prohibited the translation of the Bible into the languages of the people.[2]

Yet some people risked their lives to spread the Word anyway. In the pre-reformation period, the Albigenses translated the New Testament into Provencal; the Waldensians translated it into French; and John Wycliffe translated it into English.

Wycliffe's work, in particular, was important. John Foxe, in his *Book of Martyrs,* describes Wycliffe's translation of 1384 as having an effect "akin to the bright light of the sun bursting forth after a total eclipse."

A whole series of translations in European languages then began to appear, and the distribution of Scripture was given a tremendous boost by the technological breakthroughs in printing developed by Johann Gutenberg in the last half of the fifteenth century. Gutenberg is said to have been specifically concerned about the distribution of the Bible: "God suffers because of the great multitudes whom His Sacred Word cannot reach."[3]

These early translators, publishers, and distributors of the Bible all suffered greatly because of their efforts to make the Scripture available to people who wanted it. They had to resort to some rather "illegal" methods, both in defiance of the church hierarchy and also in defiance of civil authorities.

Englishman William Tyndale, whose smuggling efforts have probably done more for the availability of the English-language Bible than any person in history, is an example of someone who had to use expedient methods. Tyndale, whose brief but effective life lasted from 1494 until he was executed in 1536, realized that lay people had no way of reading the Bible for themselves. He began to see, according to his own statement, that "it was impossible to establish the lay people in any truth except the Scriptures were plainly laid before their eyes in their mother tongue." This courageous man began a daring effort not only to translate the Bible from the original Hebrew and Greek but also to have the Scriptures printed. He first needed a sponsor and the person he thought most likely to help him was the bishop of London, Cuthbert Tunstall.

Tyndale wanted Tunstall to authorize the translation and then have it printed. But the bishop was dead set against it. He said, "We had better be without God's law than have it translated into the common tongue of the people."

So Tyndale went to Germany, where the Reformation was fast gaining ground. He met with Luther, who was then translating the Bible into vernacular German in Wittenberg. Even though forced to constantly move from place to place, Tyndale completed his own New Testament translation. In the town of Worms, he found a printer daring enough to risk certain death for printing the banned English translation of the Scriptures, and the first printing came off the press in 1525. In the following year, a second printing was run in a smaller format. Altogether, some 15,000 copies of this first edition were printed.

Tyndale now had to find a way to get them back into England. Fortunately, some Dutch merchants came to his assistance and smuggled the precious contraband in sacks of flour, bundles of flax, and bales of cotton. As Tyndale had expected, the laity grabbed up these first printed English New Testaments, which were bound with false covers to hide their contents.

Today only a part of one copy of the first edition exists and only two copies of the 1526 edition, because after distribution they were either confiscated and burned, or so eagerly read that the copies disintegrated with use. (By the year 1534, Tyndale had completed a revision that eventually was used as the basis for the King James Version of 1611.)

The bishop of London was understandably upset when Tyndale's Bibles began to appear, and right in front of St. Paul's Cross, London, he publicly burned as many copies as he could get his hands on. Not surprisingly, it wasn't easy to get copies to burn. Those who had them treasured them rather highly! Because Tunstall felt he needed more copies to burn, he found a merchant who indicated he could deliver more copies. This merchant was actually a friend of Tyndale's and quickly reported to him that he had a buyer for his Bibles.

"Who is he?" questioned Tyndale.

"The bishop of London."

Rather than being upset, Tyndale was overjoyed. He knew he could use the bishop's money to finance more printings and to cover some of his debts. He could sell all the copies left from the first printings, pay his debts, and cover the cost of printing the revised translation. With this strange deal, Tyndale got his money, the bishop his Bibles to burn, and the merchant his commission!

Eventually, Tyndale was trapped by authorities. These authorities, who were on the side of the English government, imprisoned him at Vilvorde, a castle just a few miles north of Brussels in Belgium. And in 1536, Tyndale was found guilty of spreading heresy; he was strangled and his body burned at the stake. Before he died, he prayed, "Lord, open the King of England's eyes."

Although he didn't know it at the time, God had already answered his prayer. In 1535, a complete English Bible began to circulate in England with the approval of King Henry VIII. It included Tyndale's New Testament and his partial translation of the Old Testament! Even more ironic was the fact that on the title page of the fourth and succeeding editions (1539–1541) of the "The Great Bible," it stated the Bible was being distributed under the auspices of Cuthbert Tunstall, bishop of London—the very cleric who once condemned and burned Tyndale's "common tongue" Bible; the same man who was really responsible for Tyndale's being martyred. Tunstall had finally been forced to endorse God's Word in the language of the people. But it took a dedicated "law breaker" to bring this about.

Pioneers in the modern missionary movement also suffered in order to take the Word of God into other countries. William Carey, the father of modern missions, discovered the British East India Company would not allow missionaries on board its ships and forbade him to enter India. Carey had to be smuggled into the free territory of Serampore by Danish sailors. Ultimately, he was responsible for organizing a unique translation team which, by 1832, had produced Bibles or portions of Scripture in forty-four languages and dialects of India.

Missionary Robert Morrison encountered a similar problem when the East India Company refused to take him to China. As a result, he had to travel from London to New York in order to sail on an American ship around South America to Canton.

Morrison knew that if the Chinese were to learn about Jesus Christ and to follow Him, they would have to have an accurate translation of the Bible in their own language. Although the Scriptures were introduced to China by Nestorian Christians as early as the seventh century, and again some centuries later by Roman Catholic missionaries, there was no evidence that a Chinese translation had ever been made. Certainly no Scripture portions had ever circulated widely.

Morrison worked under incredibly difficult circumstances to translate the whole Bible into Chinese.

> During the trading season he was compelled to live within a crowded and constructed factory site of only a few acres' extent on the outskirts of a city whose oppressive temperature sapped every European's strength; when the merchant ships sailed all foreigners had to leave Canton for Portuguese Macao, the only city where permanent residence was permitted. The Chinese government forbade, on pain of death, all Chinese to teach language to foreigners. The teacher who did venture to instruct Morrison carried poison on his person so as always to be ready to commit suicide should he be discovered.[4]

One night about six years into the project, Morrison and his language assistant, A-ko, were working secretly in their dimly lit room. The windows were covered to prevent the escape of light. A-ko was amazed at this Englishman's tenacity. He pointed out that Morrison, a "missionary in disguise," would certainly be killed by the authorities if they discovered what he was doing. He questioned, "Do you not see that our land and the hearts of our people are utterly closed to you and your religion?"

"Yes," Morrison replied, "but it is written, 'Is not my word like a fire? said the Lord; and like a hammer that breaketh the rock in pieces?' This Bible is the one thing that can burn gates of brass and penetrate walls of rock. I cannot preach to the people but I can secretly translate and circulate this Book, with the confidence that its divine message will operate with divine power."[5]

What a statement of faith! No wonder Robert Morrison went on to surmount mountainous hardships and complete his translation in 1823—sixteen long years after his arrival in China. During those years, A-ko became his first convert.

Translation was one hurdle for Morrison, but distribution became a greater one. Because Christianity was a proscribed religion, and the printing and circulation of Scriptures absolutely forbidden, attempts to induce Cantonese booksellers to distribute the new translation were largely unsuccessful.

When the printing of the early translation began, the Chinese who cut the wooden blocks from which the first editions were printed were, to use Morrison's word, "hunted from place to place and sometimes seized." When the Book of Acts—the earliest portion—was issued in 1810, the printers pasted a false label over the paper covers before delivering the books to the booksellers. As more and more of these portions appeared, the government decreed death to any European spreading books on the Christian religion and exile to North Manchuria to any Chinese deluded by them.[6]

In the first twenty-five years, Chinese New Testaments were circulated largely in centers outside China, such as Singapore and Malacca. But some Christian workers traveled in junks up the coast of China, distributing many thousands of testaments and portions in coastal cities.

An interesting parallel might well be drawn between the position in China during these thirty-three years, 1807-1840, and the position now. Then as now foreign nations were suspect and must be kept out at all costs. The Bible Society, however, refused to believe that the influence of the Scriptures could be circumscribed and sought and found an entrance in various ways into this forbidden land.[7]

After the Opium War brought an opening to foreign missionaries, the next one-hundred years saw Bibles distributed to the farthest corners of China. But communism brought a reversal, and today the Bible is as officially unwelcome as it was prior to 1840. Once again, deliveries of Bibles have to be made in secret, using methods similar to when it was first translated, printed, and distributed in China. We keep taking Bibles in, even when this is forbidden, because we firmly believe, as Morrison did, that the Bible's divine message will operate with divine power as we get it through the barriers raised by Satan.

This world is an enemy-occupied territory filled with souls to whom Christ holds rightful claim. Under Christ's command, we invade countries by any means that will help us to get in with the Word of God.

We are under obligation to obey God rather than men. His commandment is: "Go!" Whenever we dally with this command, or compromise, or debate its morality, we deny God His right to rule the world. That's exactly when the devil is in command.

It's time we use Holy Spirit boldness to see the nations as God sees them. We are not facing an ethical issue but a loyalty issue. If we are true followers of the Lord Jesus Christ, we will go into *all* the world because He sends us. We need no welcome, we need no invitation, we need no permission from the government, although we are, as Christians, naturally prepared to respect normal procedures whenever that means we can be granted official permission to carry Bibles in and witness in a country. We need no red-carpet treatment, we need no VIP reception—unless it means Very Important Prisoner for Christ's sake!

The Targets of Satan's Attacks

Some critics object that our aggressiveness only makes things harder for the local believers we are trying to help. Consider two facts. First, in many places the situation could not be any more difficult than it already is, and our coming in gives the stimulus these oppressed brothers need to keep hope alive and courageous witnessing going forward. Second, I and every worker in Open Doors know that we are to sacrifice ourselves, even to die if need be, rather than to do or say anything that might implicate local believers and get them into trouble with the authorities.

What is so hard for people who live in freedom to realize is that dear Christians in restricted countries are literally hazarding their lives for the gospel every day. The records of intimidation, persecution, imprisonment, torture and execution are so abundant they constitute an international scandal. At Open Doors we surely do not knowingly make their lot worse.

The moves we make to help them are always in response to their own intense pleadings for the very aid we bring. We take every precaution to minimize the danger to them and do not go rushing into any situation without receiving their careful instructions and without honoring their local arrangements. They, in turn, are deeply concerned not to jeopardize the effectiveness of our ministries; together we labor to preserve and protect each other as we go about the Lord's business.

To meet their many needs, we supply much more than Bibles, precious and primary as these may be. We also provide food, clothing, and money in cases of physical distress. For an evangelist in Romania, for instance, we provided a car to make his ministry more effective. For a brother in Yugoslavia, we gave money to help purchase a building where he could hold Christian meetings under the strict laws then in force. In every situation, we labor to preserve the local church and extend its work.

All the time I am saying "we," I refer to scores of fellowworkers of mine who operate individually, or as small teams, permanently or on a short-term basis, under the administration of our mission. Ours is not a one-man effort although I seem to have been singled out for special publicity. While our international headquarters are in my native Holland, the Open Doors mission has offices all over the world.

We work not only in countries closed by communism but also in the even more difficult (or maybe I should say more tightly closed) Islamic countries. Currently, we are also involved in countries where there is revolutionary activity or in those threatened with revolution.

Our work takes us into countries where there is persecution, where the gospel is not allowed to be preached openly, where Bible distribution is limited or even completely forbidden. We can say that our work *begins* wherever totalitarian governments forbid missionary work.

That is also the reason why we can publicly describe only a fraction of our work—or even where we work! We are, in more than one respect, a faith mission; and while missions and evangelical leaders speak of a "shrinking free world," we in Open Doors see our mission field becoming continually larger. Alas, I should add, because that means there are more and more victims of dictatorships, countlessly more victims of war and violence, plus overflowing prisons and labor camps. Large parts of the world population cannot accept or approve on religious or moral grounds the revolution that took place in their country. These people remain prisoners of conscience and such lessening of freedom always means more persecution for the church.

Our methods of taking the Bible into places where it is not available nor permitted is actually very close to the New Testament concept of transmitting the Word of God. In our Western nations, we enjoy the rare privilege of seeing people come to us for the message. We even wait for them to come and we put up special buildings for them to come to. Then we open the doors and welcome them with a smile.

Such methods make me feel that we've responded very wrongly to Jesus' announced intention to make us "fishers of men." We have made a beautiful net of our church buildings and have set it up on the shore waiting for the fish to jump in of their own accord!

Our pattern of waiting for people to come to us is exactly the reverse of the Great Commission. Because we have done it this way for so long we have even begun to question the original way that God intended for it to be. What a topsy-turvy world we live in!

A brother named George Young has given a stirring call for a return to God's methods in the book, *The Living Christ in Modern China:*

> The evangelism that we practice must be that healthy, balanced evangelism of Jesus, which seeks the salvation of the whole man—mind, body, and soul. The revival that we pray for must be spiritual and social; it must go deep in cleansing the moral life and wide in transforming the social and economic life of our nation. It must be a revival of apostolic preaching and of apostolic practicing of Christianity. It is my deep personal conviction that the answer to the challenge of Communism is a rebirth of Apostolic Christianity with a flaming evangelism and the Kingdom of God community life which will be more revolutionary than that of the Communists.[8]

That is the issue. We must have the courage, the Holy Spirit boldness, to live a life that is more revolutionary than that of *any* non-Christian faith. The Lord will give us the courage to work like commandos if we want Him to, but we must go and carry out His commission.

The command has been given by the risen Lord and the call

is clear: prepare for spiritual battle! Let's go in Jesus' name and do it! We can do it because ever since He first issued the orders, Jesus has given to every generation the ability, the strength, the manpower, and the opportunity to do it.

Although every generation has failed in some way, the first generation almost accomplished it. Almost! In our generation we don't need to fail. We can fulfill the commission because Jesus Christ is the same yesterday, today, and forever. He who holds all authority in heaven and on earth has authorized us to advance on His enemy everywhere, including across every "closed" border. He still endues us with the power of the Holy Spirit that we might be witnesses to the uttermost parts of the earth.

"Awake, and strengthen what remains" (Rev. 3:2). That is the watchword of our ministry to fellow-believers in Eastern Europe, China, Africa, and now in Latin America as well. What constrains us is the love of Christ; for love, the Word of God tells us, is the fulfillment of all divine commands. I want others to have the one who makes me happy—Jesus. I want others to have what makes me grow spiritually—the Bible.

The God of miracles will bring it to pass!

6
We Should Expect Suffering

Up to now we have used a lot of illustrations that refer to suffering and persecution. The possibility of suffering is not a happy prospect for many Christians. As a matter of fact, however, it should be regarded as an integral component of the Christian life.

Look at the apostles. In Acts 14 Paul and Barnabas go on a preaching tour. "When they had preached the gospel to that city [Derbe] and had made many disciples, they returned to Lystra and to Iconium and to Antioch, strengthening the souls of the disciples, exhorting them to continue in the faith" (Acts 14:21–22). Paul and Barnabas had gone from city to city; they had preached the simple gospel.

But the results Paul got were amazing! And that was not because people were more open to the gospel in Paul's time than in our time. I refuse to believe that this is a different time as far as man's ability to respond to the gospel is concerned. People are people everywhere and always. People everywhere need God. People everywhere need peace and forgiveness. People everywhere need healing and salvation.

The record in Acts says that when Paul and Barnabas preached in those cities, they made many disciples. This matter of making disciples is an important point. Are we in our ministries making disciples? Or are we merely winning souls? Is our greatest satisfaction only in gaining impressive statistics for the number of souls who have made a decision? I'm afraid too many of us are working far too much for statistics.

Paul was an evangelist who made many disciples. C.T. Studd, that marvelous missionary who founded the Worldwide Evangelization Crusade, said it takes only 1 percent of effort to win a person for Christ, but it takes 99 percent of effort to make a disciple of him. God wants and uses disciples! A disciple is one who is disciplined by Jesus Christ; one who is equipped by God to do God's work, in God's time, with God's methods, to God's honor. A disciple knows his Bible, and he knows how to pray. He knows how to have power and authority over the invisible world.

Although Paul had already made disciples, he went back because they needed to be strengthened. This was part of the process. How did he strengthen them? He told them "through many tribulations we must enter the kingdom of God" (Acts 14:22).

Now, Paul, you are not a good psychologist! You don't encourage people by saying that they're going to have a rough time. Surely, Paul, there must be a different method and a different message! But Paul says, "No, there is a price you have to pay."

One of my favorite books, an all-time best-seller, is *Pilgrim's Progress,* written by John Bunyan. Bunyan was a tinker, a mender of pots in the village of Bedford, England. He was a very humble man, but once he came to know the Lord he was an earnest preacher of the gospel.

During his time, England was not favorably disposed to such independent evangelists, and Bunyan was imprisoned for preaching the gospel. With the exception of a few days, he spent nearly twelve years in the Bedford jail, until he was finally freed by the Declaration of Indulgence. "As the law stood he had indisputably broken it, and he expressed his determination, respectfully but firmly, to take the first opportunity of breaking it again. 'I told them that if I was out of prison today I would preach the gospel again tomorrow by the help of God.' "[1]

Bunyan recognized the truth that the apostle Paul also preached: there is a price to pay for being a Christian.

Some years ago I had an evangelistic campaign in the Baptist churches of Budapest. The crowds were so great every night that we had to move from church to church for security reasons. Supposedly, I was not allowed to preach, but only to give greetings. But I had many greetings! From my family, from my home church, I even had greetings from the apostle Paul, and he had written them down for me so I could read them to the people! Then I would say that even the apostle Peter thought Paul's epistles were hard to understand, so I would have to explain his greetings as well.

Even though I was not preaching, only explaining Paul's greetings, it was amazing to see how many people came forward every night to accept Christ as Savior.

One evening after a service, we went to the home of one of the leading pastors. As we were sitting there with about a dozen pastors and elders of the church, the door opened and an old friend of mine came in, a pastor from Romania. I was happy to see him, because when I had been in Romania previously, he had been in prison. In fact, he had often been in prison, but now he was free again, traveling and preaching.

You have no idea what a joy it is to embrace a brother just come out of prison. Every time I do it I feel so small and unworthy because I have never paid the price they have paid.

This brother sat down in our group and looked expectantly at me. But I was quiet, too, although I had been speaking to the group. When you are in the presence of a man who has paid a price for his faith, you do not want to talk, you want to listen. You want to learn, because you know, deep in your heart, that one day you will have to pay the price too, and the more we can learn from the saints of God the better it will be for us in such a time. (That's why it is so important to study the Scriptures, to study the biographies of men and women of God in the Bible, and to study the biographies of saints throughout the history of the church.)

Finally this brother broke the silence. "Andrew, are there any pastors in prison in Holland?"

What a strange question, I thought. Of course there are no pastors in prison in Holland! Why should any of us be in prison? Everything is allowed in my country. We can buy and sell Bibles, even give them away. We can give out Christian books, and preach on the radio and television. I do both in my own country. We can stand on the street corners and speak about Jesus, invite our neighbors to come to church with us on Sunday, and witness to our colleagues and fellow students. Of course we don't do these things, but we could do them if we wanted to. We have so much liberty, why should any of us be in prison?

That's what I told my dear brother who had just come out of prison. My pastor friend was very quiet for a long time. He turned again to me with a question. This time it was an even more piercing question, "Why not?"

"I think it is simply because we do not use all of the opportunities God gives us," I replied.

He thought for a while, then said, "Andrew, I have one more question. What do you do with 2 Timothy 3:12?"

As I read "Indeed all who desire to live a godly life in Christ Jesus will be persecuted," I felt so ashamed. We in Holland are not being persecuted. Very possibly the Christians in your country are not being persecuted. I read it again and thought maybe it meant that only some people will be persecuted. But it said *all*. I thought maybe it was only for the people living in communistic countries, or that maybe it was for Christians living in Muslim societies, but that surely it could not apply to those of us living in so-called Christian countries. No, it said *all* who truly want to follow Jesus Christ will have to pay a personal price for that privilege. Revelation chapters two and three say the same thing.

Finally I said, "Brother, please forgive me. We do nothing with that verse." I knew deep in my heart there were many verses with which we do nothing because we don't want the Bible to interfere with our Christianity. We have actually built our "Christian" philosophy upon a handful of carefully selected verses.

Paul said that through much persecution and tribulation we must enter the kingdom of God. But then, don't forget, Paul was instructing disciples, he was not speaking merely to souls. God made a whole man, body, soul, and spirit. The Lordship of Christ involves the whole of us, all that we are and all that we have.

We have a message to the church today: we cannot overcome with God if we are not willing to pay the price. Revelation 12: 11 says our brethren have conquered the devil. How did they do it?

There are three important elements in conquering the devil.

First, "they have conquered him by the blood of the Lamb." All victorious believers are based upon that one foundation, Jesus Christ, the Christ who came to die for us on the cross.

Second, they overcame him "by the word of their testimony." Yes, if you only do good things without telling people why you do good things, then you are not building with God. You must pass on the message of redemption even where this is not allowed.

We must preach what we practice!

The third element is this: "They loved not their lives even

unto death." That is God's message to the church today. The question is, are you really willing to lay down your life? Give God your answer, for this is a part of God's training of you as a disciple.

We must practice what we preach!

In Acts chapter 17, Paul and his evangelistic team witnessed and proclaimed Christ in the city of Thessalonica. The city council had gathered in utter panic when they heard Paul was in their city. They were afraid of Paul! They said, "These men who have turned the world upside down have come here also" (Acts 17:6).

I love that statement! It demonstrates that the enemies of Christ are afraid of the gospel. So many countries today do not want the Bible because they are afraid of its political influence. They know that the gospel, as lived out by dedicated Christians, has greater power than their ideologies. A dedicated Christian stands out from the crowd. So many ideologies depend on mass movements which really involve mob psychology, but Christians are not blind followers of a set of dogmas. They know what they believe and live it out.

The leaders in Ephesus said, "These men who have turned the world upside down have come here also." Think about it for a minute. Is what they say true? No, it is not true. These enemies of Christ serve the devil. The devil is the father of lies; therefore his servants tell lies. The apostles never turned the world upside down; that's what the devil had done long before. The apostles had come to turn the world right-side up! Yes, they would turn the world around—to the right way. We must not accept any accusation that would suggest we who proclaim the truth in Christ are the cause of unrest in the world.

Once while traveling in Eastern Europe, I was arrested and taken to the secret police headquarters for interrogation. Whenever I am arrested, I preach as powerfully as I can to those who interrogate me. I reason that they'll be afraid I might convert them all, so they will kick me out. This time I said, "Sir, listen to me. You know that I am doing a good work in your country. And you know that the Christians in your country are the best citizens. They are the best workers in your country. They are the most honest people in your country. It's all because they believe in the Lord Jesus Christ."

That secret police officer actually helped me to get out of the country! He knew that what I said was true. In every country I know of, Christians are the most productive, honest citizens there. Today's authorities show a deep inner conflict, just as the authorities did in Paul's day.

The reason is obvious. "They are all acting against the decrees of Caesar, saying that there is another king, Jesus" (Acts 17:17). Paul preached another King! Paul preached a higher law than that of men.

It is very important that we understand this today. We live in a complex world where there are many different laws and ideologies that control many different nations. And we wonder if the relatively simple choice of the New Testament saints might not have been easier to live with.

But we must remember that the situation in which the apostle John lived out his last days most resembles the conditions of believers in Russia or China rather than in free countries. This greatly encourages me because it offers further evidence of the long sweep of the spiritual struggle over the centuries. Even those who do not see that struggle in the same way I do still play a part in it.

Sometimes I do wonder whose side they are really on.

7
Our Upside-Down World

When Paul and his evangelistic group proclaimed Jesus as Lord in Thessalonica, the city council was told: "These men who have turned the world upside down have come here also" (Acts 17:6).

That statement was not really true. The devil had turned the world upside down, and these men had come to put it straight again! People willing to live that radically for Christ are, of course, resented by those responsible for governing this world. The whole world is in the grip of the evil one, so it's not unusual for its rulers to be in his grip also (1 John 3:19).

Thus, when Jesus sends us to make disciples of all nations, the assumption must be that the people of those nations are not already disciples of His. The reality of the world's situation is aptly summarized by Watchman Nee, a great Chinese saint who died in June 1972, after more than twenty years in a Chinese prison. The entry for January 10 in his devotional book, *A Table in the Wilderness,* is a little commentary on Psalm 2:1, which asks "Why do the nations rage?"

The answer is supplied at once: it is because the rulers take council together against the Lord and against His anointed. However violent the hostility between them, world governments are at heart united on the wrong thing—they are against

66

the reign of Christ. We look upon the nations as some of them bad, some good. But Scripture points us to the prince of this world behind them all. Prompted by him, earth's rulers today seek only absolute freedom from sanctions imposed by the law of Christ. They want no more love, no more humility, no more truth. Let us break these bands asunder, they cry, and cast away the cords from us. At this point alone in all Scripture is God said to laugh. His King is already on His holy hill. The early Church was very much aware of Christ's dominion. More than ever today do we need to remember it. Soon, maybe in our lifetime, He will shepherd the nations with a rod of iron. Our task is to plead with men to be wise, to put their trust in Him.[1]

For the student of God's Word, hostility toward the church of Jesus Christ should come as no surprise. The Bible makes it clear that the nations of this world simply are not for Christ. In Luke 21:12, in speaking of the end-time with its earthquakes, famines, pestilences, and other signs from heaven, Jesus says: " 'But before all this they will lay their hands on you and persecute you, delivering you up to the synagogues and prisons, and you will be brought before kings and governors for my name's sake.' "

Jesus warns us that religious persecution will be carried out in the name of authority. We see again how upside down this world can become! Surely it's time we carried out our commission and put it right.

We are pitted against systems in the service of the devil. Their aim is to prevent the kingdom of God from coming to this world. Those in the service of the devil have suppressed the truth, killed pastors, imprisoned believers, and burned churches.

Add to this the common conditions of poverty, violence, and uncertainty, and you have the ingredients for revolution. The perfect breeding ground for revolution is man at war—at war with himself, with society, with other races, with labor conditions, with other religious factions, even with poverty and injustice. Never before have the conditions been more ripe for revolution.

When I use the word revolution I refer to those people in whatever cause who would destroy the church as an effective witness to men and women. These people say, "Christianity and its ideas have been around for all these years, but look at the mess we have." This sort of revolution offers a new world order based on a denial of God as an outmoded myth. It is a movement to capture men's minds and convince them that the problems of the world can only be solved by destroying the church with all its values and teachings.

Alexander Solzhenitsyn, the exiled Soviet novelist, commenting on the U. S. Supreme Court's ban on school prayers, said: "When prayers in school are forbidden even in a free country, it is not much more tolerable than in Communist countries, only in that it lacks the hammering-in of atheism." The aim is always the same, you see: to destroy the church—either through physical force, intellectual arguments, or social ridicule—and to tear people away from Christian values so they have no source of authority but the revolution itself.

In the revolution, hatred finds an outlet to destroy the church. The revolution seeks to point to people's miseries and blame everything on Christianity. So men join the revolution to seek a new world at whatever cost in blood and suffering.

In Havana, Cuba, I once saw a quotation from Che Guevara emblazoned on the wall of a hospital: "If this revolution is not aimed at changing people, then I am not interested." That is the power of revolution—to change men by winning their minds.

This sort of revolution, however, is not necessarily communistic, though it can be. Worldwide communism is part of the revolution and one of the major forces of it, but the revolution has many other faces. In a particular case, it may not take the form of communism at all. It may merely be an agent of materialism in a given country or ethnic group, or an aspect of existential philosophy on a university campus.

A ruler such as the now-deposed Idi Amin of Uganda would stoutly insist that he was not a Communist, that he sought only an independent course for his country. Amin's loyalty lay only with himself and his tribe. Nevertheless, his ruthless campaign against the church placed him squarely in the frontlines of the godless revolution of which I speak. The revolution preaches that violence is an acceptable method of gaining power and that individual human beings are expendable when their deaths will aid a particular movement.

The nature of the revolution is essentially ideological, not political or military. The revolution often spreads effectively through infiltration and control of educational systems, the news media, and even religious institutions. Because it is a spiritual movement at its root, it must be fought with spiritual weapons. Yet America and the West have often seemed to oppose the spread of the revolution primarily with military means. This approach seldom works when opposing an ideological cause.

In ideological conflicts, the more enemies one kills, the more martyrs one provides for his cause. That is exactly what he wants. We can learn this lesson from the sad experience of the Vietnam war. The South seemed to have overwhelming military support; but the revolution won the ideological war and the fall of Saigon was inevitable.

Because so much of the unconventional ministry of our Open Doors with Brother Andrew team takes place in Communist-dominated countries, some label us anti-Communist. That label is not true in a political sense, but in a spiritual sense it may be correct as we seek to overcome the atheistic and anti-God influences of a Marxist regime.

The struggle is a spiritual one because communism is a religion! The clearest and most concise statement I have ever seen on this fact comes from David Adeney, who worked with university students in China until it fell to the forces of Mao Tse-tung. Even though many things have changed since then—Stalin is dead, Mao Tse-tung is dead—communism has not changed, so Adeney's statements are still valid.

Communism—a religion

To students full of youthful idealism Communism seemed to offer the chance to build a new society. It took the place of all other ideologies and religious beliefs. While claiming to be completely materialistic, Communist leaders recognized that they must produce spiritual qualities in their followers. For this reason we find in Communism a counterfeit for almost every Christian doctrine. The system of materialism has itself become a kind of pseudo-religion. The marks of a religion are usually given as: (1) a doctrine of God, (2) a doctrine of a messiah or chosen revealer of God, (3) a doctrine of man, (4) a doctrine of salvation, and (5) a doctrine of ultimate destiny. Chinese Communism bears all these marks.

God

The true Communist denies the existence of both God and the devil, although he may not always be consistent... Denial of God is indeed basic to all Communist belief, and small children in the schools are taught to sing, "There is no God, there is no devil, so do not be afraid." The Communist gospel says that God is not love, God is not personal; rather God is inevitable necessity which moves in history to redeem men's bodies and minds from the slavery of hunger and injustice... Thus, while Communism has no concept of God as such, it supplies a substitute. Man in society becomes the God of Communism.

Our Upside-Down World

The messiah

The Communist equivalent of a saviour or messiah is a composite man, Marx-Lenin-Stalin-Mao, who is regarded as the revealer of the way and the truth of history and who alone has the words of economic life...and is regarded as the giver of new life, the saviour from the oppression of the past and the source of all inspiration for the building of the New China.

Man

The Communist doctrine of man is built upon the shaky foundation of evolutionary theory, and one of the first courses of study compulsory for every student is that which deals with "the development of society." The object of this course is to prove that all progress is the result of "struggle."...Man by scientific means has created the manifold comforts which have transformed the material world and will bring about a new social order by the united effort of the proletariat...The Communists were indeed seeking to establish the kingdom of man, and we frequently would hear the slogan, "Do not worship earth, do not worship heaven, only worship the effort of the people."

Salvation

Enthusiastic Communist students would sometimes describe their conversion to Communism in terms similar to those used by Christians to describe salvation...Communist salvation involves becoming "a new man." It is described as coming out of the darkness of superstition into the light....

But the Communist concept of salvation differs from the Christian one in that it has no connection with sin in the biblical sense. Communism has no absolute moral standards, for what is wrong today can be right tomorrow and always the end justifies the means. In the Marxist ethic, there is no individual

71

moral responsibility because evil is seen as an accident caused by external factors such as ignorance, social inequalities, and man's animal origin. Sin is the result of man's alienation from ultimate reality, which is seen in materialistic terms. Man is alienated from the means of production and from the fruits of production which are rightfully his. Evil can be overthrown only when private ownership is destroyed. From this it is clear that evil springs from the capitalist form of economic relations. When these forms are changed in a classless society, sin is removed. In this utopia lies ultimate salvation. Until the unjust structures are destroyed, man is not responsible for his personal sins. Morever, in attaining the classless society, no action is considered evil if it furthers the revolution....

Communist salvation is concerned with the transformation of the man and of the society in which he lives. It is to be brought about by social, psychological, and educational means. Because of their great emphasis upon scientific technology, the Communists constantly confuse technical possibilities with moral capacity.

Ultimate destiny
The Communists believe that they "will make all things new." They look forward to a new earth permeated not by Christian righteousness but by the classless society. This society is to be completely balanced economically and free from all injustice and inequality....

For the Communist there is no future life for the individual and therefore the only form of judgment which he recognizes is that which comes in this life. His reward is the satisfaction that he is having a part in the on-going process which will bring about the future Communist society that later generations will enjoy.

The Communist scriptures

China's millions have become the people of the book. Millions of copies of the Little Red Book and other more extensive selections from the writings of Mao Tse-tung have been used to inspire and control and unite the peoples of China....

There is to be "living study and living use" so that study and application are combined. Through literacy campaigns and the skillful use of mass media combined with multitudes of small discussion groups and the enthusiastic testimony of people from all walks of life, it won the hearts and minds of the people....

Evangelism

Communistic "evangelistic" methods are strikingly familiar.... The Communists fully realize the value of testimony. Not only does it strengthen the convert, but it also has a powerful effect in bolstering the morale of their followers and persuading those who are wavering.... Mass meetings and other forms of propaganda are not nearly so effective as the personal work done by an enthusiastic believer in scientific materialism....

It would be a great mistake to regard Communism merely as a political system. Communism is not only a religion, it is also a dynamic missionary movement aspiring to the conquest of the whole world. Although it professes to be entirely materialistic, scorning idealism and the things of the spirit, it finds itself compelled to cater to the spiritual needs of its followers. It attempts to provide a substitute not only for Christian doctrine and experience but also for many of the methods and activities used in the church. Indeed Communists have often adapted Christian methods and have proved themselves to be more thorough and efficient in using them than the Christians from whom they were borrowed.[2]

We must remember that the revolution does not always operate under the name of communism. It often takes the form of nationalism or anti-imperialism.

As a matter of fact, this is the first time in history that there has been a single concerted effort—we call it revolution—to wipe out the entire church. To be sure, there has always been opposition and persecution directed at the church, but never on the scale we see it now. Some assert that more people have died for their faith in our generation than in the twenty previous centuries of Christianity put together. About half the world today, under the cloak of communism, is united in one big deliberate effort to annihilate Christ's church.

The fact that communism is both a religion and that it is dedicated to destroying the church requires me to explain more fully its bearing on the special work that the Lord has called me and my team and the Open Doors ministry to do.

The thing that got me going nearly thirty years ago was hearing that the Communist youth movement had ninety-seven million members. Since fanatical Communist youth leaders often put severe pressure on young people to join the party, maybe that is why the number in those young Communist leagues has swelled to more than 120 million members, making it by far the largest such organization in the world. As faithful followers of the party line, they are being trained for world revolution and they are going to risk their lives to succeed.

Years ago, when Kruschchev was still in power, he stood at Red Square in Moscow and spoke with scriptural-sounding words to the massed troops of the army: "You are all dead men!", implying that they had already lost their lives to the cause. Then he added: "Now, go into the world and prove it!" In effect, Christ said almost the same thing to His disciples.

Yes, communism is a religion; therefore, our battle is spiritual. I do not believe military action can smash the power of communism because it has two elements that make it extremely resilient: a common foe and a purpose for the future.

Without an enemy, communism cannot exist. If Marxist leaders do not have an enemy, they make one, as Mao did when he started his cultural revolution. He had to create a conflict to keep communism vital in China. There must be a conflict, a struggle, in order to maintain control of the masses.

As far as China is concerned, both America and Russia are, or have been, enemy number one. Even if China reconciled with all parties, something else would have to become a target of conflict. There must be an enemy.

It's frightening to see how far they will go in this, even creating an enemy within their own circles as Mao did. His fellow-ministers in Peking, with whom he had fought side by side for fifty years, became his enemies so his people might be stirred to unity. It was fearful to watch that. We can never have peace in the world as long as there is such an ideology at work, nor will we ever conquer communism as long as we put our trust in men. It can be opposed and overcome only by another spiritual power: the church of Jesus Christ!

Therefore, in those countries where the church of the Lord Jesus Christ is being suppressed, persecuted, and almost wiped out (as it seemed once in China, and now seems in Albania), believers are under divine obligation to step in and do things their governments object to and consider illegal. We have got to do it for the sake of Christ and for the sake of the whole world for which He died.

But, we do not have time on our side, because the world is a much smaller place than it was a hundred years ago. Whatever happens in one country politically is going to affect other countries profoundly. There is no longer room for attitudes like, "My country, right or wrong." It's a different world now, and narrow isolationism won't make us safe from turmoil elsewhere.

We need to understand that what happens to our brethren

in El Salvador or Afghanistan, Cuba or Vietnam has a direct correlation on the progress of spiritual battles in our own countries. Can we expect God to protect us and our interests when we are unconcerned about the struggles of our brothers and sisters outside our frontiers?

For example, we cannot expect to win on the abortion issue at home, unless we are also concerned about what happens to our brothers in Russia. The two issues are linked. The acceptance of abortion shows our failure in the spiritual battle to protect the family unit, strengthen our educational system, and infuse our pulpits with morality and dynamism.

We need to strengthen the concept of the worldwide body of Christ because such a concept gives us a sense of responsibility and a greater awareness of a world in need. A sense of unity gives us hope and the assurance that God will work.

That is the position of Open Doors. We believe that we have a great commission and command to go in and preach Christ's deliverance to the captives, to win others to the Lord, yes, to win Communists for Christ!

It is a spiritual battle. Therefore we must be spiritual people, and we must see the spiritual principles involved in the conflict before we can effectively minister in this world.

Dr. Boris P. Dotsenko, a Russian nuclear scientist who defected to Canada in 1967, correctly observes that for Communists an ideological foe is the worst enemy.[3] Their hottest hatred and fiercest persecutions are focused on Christian believers! The volume of documentation proving this is overwhelming. And the continued persecution is a scandal that has been brought to the attention of international councils time after time to no avail.

Several years ago, the Norwegian Parliament (Storting) conducted a full debate on the persecution of Christians behind the Iron Curtain, the first time any national body had done such a thing. The parliamentary question was "Can anything be done on the part of Norway to end the persecution of Christians on the other side of the Iron Curtain?"

During the speeches made by leading members of Norway's political parties, the reliability and credibility of reports of persecutions were never questioned. The records told of imprisonment, children separated from parents, meetings disrupted, and homes destroyed.

Karl Aasland, Storting representative of the Center Party, observed that it was clear enough that some countries knowingly and systematically obstructed the freedom to practice one's religion. He stated he had no doubt that this was part of a policy the purpose of which was to break down and exterminate all religion. The most dangerous aspect of these destructive efforts involved the complete denial of choice to the individual and the inculcation of atheistic ideology to the children and young people.

This debate in the Storting drew from an earlier strong statement issued on the matter of persecutions by the Norwegian Convocation of Bishops. They said in part:

> Officially there prevails in these countries full freedom of religion. One should, however, realize that Christian evangelization is being restricted to such an extent that believers are deprived of the basic opportunities to witness to their faith. Christians who violate such restrictions are being punished as enemies of the state and as offenders of civil law. In reality they are, however, punished for their faith. They are punished because they take their faith seriously, and, in accordance with the Master's words, try to convert people. We would feel like traitors against the cause of the gospel itself if we forget this, if we fail to speak up against this, and if we neglect to do that which is within our power to build a worldwide opinion against this.

I am delighted that the clergy in Norway played their proper role in speaking out for a commitment to persecuted Christians. This is where so often our pastors fail in their responsibilities. They avoid preaching on tougher, less popular subjects. We need to call them back to their commission to preach the Word of God, fully and relevantly.

A recent book on the founding of America reminds us that this is the spiritual heritage of America. *The Light and the Glory* documents the role that ministers played in setting the stage for the American Revolution.

The authors attribute the moral stamina of America in those early years to men whose spiritual character had been shaped by the Great Awakening in the early eighteenth century:

> As usual, American opinion on this mounting crisis was strongly shaped by the ministers. Those men of God who were American-born and not in Crown Colonies (such as Georgia and Virginia) were becoming nearly unanimous in their support of resistance. Thanks to the Great Awakening, there was now a new generation of committed clergymen salted throughout America, many of them men of considerable spiritual depth and maturity. As the list of "intolerable acts" mounted, so did their remonstrations. It was almost as if they had George III in the front row of their congregations, and were trying to make him see the error of his ways.[4]

Now, frankly, I must confess that I am bewildered when some preachers counsel that we should not identify with the body of Christ in countries of repression. We are told we must not break inhuman and indecent laws in order to help our brothers who are being persecuted for their faith and faithfulness. That is bewildering indeed. Why should I obey laws which my fellow Christians behind the Iron Curtain are breaking and which are internationally denounced as illegal? It surely doesn't make sense to me! Who has turned the world upside down?

Let me illustrate my concern with direct reference to the matter of Bibles. Some organizations claim that Bibles are available in restricted countries. But here is the way it really works. In Romania, for instance, quite a number of Bible copies were printed—but in a translation totally unacceptable to evangelical Protestants. The government had only authorized a reprint of an ancient translation, which could be read only by priests of the Orthodox church. The edition was not even made available to Protestants!

One of the Romanian officials claimed that the distribution of Scripture was tied to the numerical strength of the congregation. He claimed that, on the average, each Romanian Orthodox Church over a period of four years received twenty-one copies of the Bible. These churches, he reported, had to send full lists of purchasers to the patriarchate, together with payment for the Bibles. That means that everyone who got a Bible was registered for possessing a Bible! In many other countries this policy has subsequently been the basis for numerous arrests!

Another touchy point involves the many tourists who have come back to the West with glowing reports about the fervent crowds that jam the services in the Moscow Baptist Church. What these travelers don't seem to comprehend is that the Communist regime tolerates a "showcase church" as a token of Soviet religious freedom. These churches put visitors' minds to rest about reports of persecution.

Soviet policy since 1944 has been to force as many Protestant groups as possible into the All-Union Council of Evangelical Christians and Baptists. This has been an open attempt by the state to tighten its control. In effect it meant the closing of many churches by "uniting" them with others. Often the church allowed to remain open was in a remote location which made it difficult for people to get to.

Men of God, such as Georgi Vins and Gennadi Kryuchkov protested: "No, we cannot do that. You go too far in cooperating with the Communist regime. We have to break away." In 1961, they started the "Initiative church," sometimes referred to as the "unregistered church." Some have wrongly called it the "underground church," but their meetings are, in fact, public, held not only in the woods but also in private homes. Meetings are sometimes attended by several thousand people. The police are often present and sometimes interfere violently; but frequently they take no action.

Since August of 1961, when the separation from the All-Union Council took place, this church has seen amazing growth. Precise figures are difficult to obtain, but its membership is now at least as large as that of the official, registered Baptist church. It is impossible to be more accurate. Some estimate that the unregistered church is at least three times the size of the registered church.

To illustrate the problem of estimating numbers, consider a report from a government source covering one Soviet province. The University of Vorones in central Russia announced that there were ninety-seven nonregistered churches in the Vorones area alone, as against eight official churches of evangelical Christians and Baptists. When Orthodox churches and other religious groups were added by the university to their census, they arrived at the enormous total of 694 active congregations.

Although Vorones boasted fifty-eight Orthodox churches before the revolution, afterward, there were only three open. By comparison, Moscow had roughly a thousand churches before the revolution and there are now less than fifty allowed to function, of which only one is evangelical. But obviously that doesn't tell the whole story, so who can tell how many groups and churches meet together in the vast city of Moscow, with its millions of inhabitants, in order to encourage and strengthen each other in the name of the Lord?

Of course, we may disagree with the policies of the official churches, and certainly with government-directed persecution. But if it were not for that persecution, then the true church today would be much smaller. As so often before in history, out of evil God still works good—and we should be encouraged that this still happens.

The way many churchmen from the West applaud the level of religious "liberty" in Russia and, by implication if not directly, condemn those who defy government policy in order to worship and witness freely, emphasizes the highly dangerous potential that one "super-church" would have so far as persecuting the real church during the end-time. I believe that no church can thrive, much less survive, if it plays games with the government according to a set of godless rules.

Dr. Dotsenko, the Russian scientist who fled the Soviet Union, suggests that "God allows...false powers to operate to test our faithfulness to Him, to check our worth for the eternal life."

He goes on: "No true power has a right to intervene in the worship of God and Christ as it is prescribed in the Scriptures. Christians ought to obey all laws that do not make them turn away from worshiping and serving God and Christ.... To accept the leadership of communism is incompatible with the true service of God. It is like accepting the assertion that the thief is the lawful owner of the things he stole."[5]

We have already pointed to the words of Jesus in Luke 21:12, in which He says that in the end-time "They will lay their hands on you and persecute you, delivering you up to the synagogues and prisons, and you will be brought before kings and governors for my name's sake." There you see again how wrong this world is, how it is indeed turned upside down! We will be delivered to "synagogues and prisons." It surely is time that we came along and put the world right.

There are two signs of the end-time: persecution and world-evangelism.

Persecution will come from political and religious opposition (Mark 13:9). Real opposition will always be against the person of Jesus Christ and all that He stands for. When Jesus speaks of wars and revolution, He says: "Do not be alarmed...the end is not yet" (Mark 13:7). Then He mentions natural disasters but warns that they, too, are only the beginning of birth pains (Mark 13:8). The prelude to the fiercest possible persecution will come when, within the body of believers (please don't say this is just the nominal church and not evangelical believers), the love of *most* (not many, not few, but *most*) will grow cold (Matt. 24:12).

This will happen simply because *all* nations will hate those who follow Jesus. I think that will include nations that up until now have seemed tolerant of Christians (Matt. 24:9). Wickedness will increase so terribly that many will not be able to stand the pressure. A sense of personal failure born of not being able to impart morality and spirituality to one's children will be followed by putting the blame on God: "If He is a God of love, how can He let this happen to us?"

Consequently many will turn away from the faith and instead of obeying the command to love each other they will betray and hate each other (Matt. 24:10). No, not the atheists, but fellow Christians will do this. "And brother will deliver up brother to death, and the father his child" (Mark 13:12).

But in both accounts of this most terrible persecution recorded in Matthew 24 and Mark 13, the middle section of both chapters states the gospel *will* be preached, and the gospel *must* be preached before the end comes (Matt. 24:14 and Mark 13:10). The Great Commission is still the watchword for Christians; not a word of it has been withdrawn. It may well be in prisons and concentration camps that the common man will hear about Jesus. It may be that during trial proceedings those who never bothered to go to church will hear the gospel. "You will stand before governors and kings for my sake, to bear testimony before them" (Mark 13:9).

The New Testament shows that interrogation rooms and the courts, not to mention prison cells, have been eminent platforms for the proclamation of the gospel. Some of the most effective sermons recorded in Scripture were given in such surroundings.

Look at these examples:

- Peter and John before the Sanhedrin (Acts 4:8–20; Acts 5:29–32).
- Stephen's speech to the Sanhedrin (Acts 7:2–53).
- Paul's defense speech in Jerusalem (Acts 22:1–21).
- Paul's testimony to the Sanhedrin (Acts 23:1–6).
- Paul's reply to Felix (Acts 24:1–21).
- Paul again before Felix, now joined by his wife Drusilla (Acts 24:25).
- Paul to King Agrippa (Acts 26:2–29).
- Paul to the Roman guards (Phil. 4:22).

Last, but not least, Paul could say he fully proclaimed the message to all the Gentiles, including his most cruel persecutor, Nero (2 Tim. 4:17).

In his running battle with the government, Paul must have had always in front of him the specific promise of Jesus found in Luke 21:14–19: "You will be hated by all men for my name's sake.... While you endure it you will gain your life." Today we do see many of these signs coming to pass, but be of good courage. If we stand up for Jesus and boldly proclaim the gospel of the Kingdom, soon the end will come!

Karl Barth, the Swiss theologian, said that in effect a government tends to move between two extremes. It's either a

Romans 13 government—a servant of God—or it is a Revelation 13 government—a beast that comes out of the sea and out of the earth. Revelation 13:10 says, "If any one is to be taken captive, to captivity he goes; if any one slays with the sword, with the sword must he be slain. Here is a call for the endurance and faith of the saints."

Jesus foresaw that the church would go through a time just like that which He went through when He died on the cross of Calvary. It is my firm conviction that the life of the church here on earth will end as the life of Jesus ended—in apparent defeat. But His apparent defeat was the greatest victory ever: "It is finished!" His "defeat" was victory.

After all of the preceding, it may occur to someone to ask: What about those Scriptures that say we are to love our enemies and to pray for them? Dr. Dotsenko again has a helpful word:

> "The true enemies of the Christian are those who are the enemies of God. All other people are his brothers and sisters in Christ. These he should love and forgive. Concerning the enemies of God, only one prayer is possible: that the Lord in His mercy will open their eyes and soften their hearts so that they will repent and accept Christ as their Lord and Saviour."[6]

His insightful distinction helps me interpret a verse I always had problems with, Psalm 139:21: "Do I not hate them that hate thee, O Lord?" We must love our enemies because we are in a horizontal relationship with them. On a human level, we never really know for sure who is right and who is wrong. Both of us can be wrong, or both can be right. David's next statement was: "I hate them with perfect hatred; I count them my enemies" (Ps. 139:22). Then after making such a harsh statement, David prayed, "Search me, O God, and know my heart! Try me and know my thoughts! And see if there be any wicked way in me and lead me in the way everlasting!" (vv. 23–24).

It is as if David said, "Lord, this is my attitude. I hate them because they hate you, but please search my heart because I'm not really sure I'm right." He presents an escape in case he is wrong. He does not state this as absolute truth; he wants God to overrule him and correct him.

You see more clearly now the true spiritual nature of this battle that engages all of our energies. When we oppose the anti-God (and anti-human) decrees of atheistic political systems such as communism, we actually wage a battle against the powers of darkness unleashed by Satan as he frantically trys to stave off his own doom assured by the glorious victory of Jesus Christ on the cross.

Jesus' claim to kingship is at the heart of this battle. It motivates us to engage in spiritual warfare and claim victory over the enemy.

8
A Closer Look at Spiritual Warfare

On a visit to Cuba, I attended a conference with pastors held on the grounds of the seminary of the Nazarene Church near Havana. One evening, a Methodist bishop spoke on Ephesians 6:12: "For we are not contending against flesh and blood, but against the principalities." Afterward, I had a talk with an Orthodox priest, a real born-again man.

"Andrew," this brother said to me, "I don't believe that with physical weapons we can do anything against communism. It is a spiritual power. Three times a day when I go to prayer, I bind all the communistic, atheistic powers in the air—and I battle in the heavens!"

"Praise the Lord, brother," I said. "That is the place to do battle. You will accomplish something for the kingdom of God, breaking down the strongholds of the devil."

That brother had discovered the only way we can effectively carry out the command of our Lord Jesus to invade enemy-occupied territory and reclaim it for God. To do spiritual battle, we must have an understanding of the invisible world.

Many Christians are confused about this. The real enemy of Christ is not some temporary political regime, however godless it may be. No, our adversary is the devil himself, and our battle is against the satanic forces that run this world.

A Closer Look at Spiritual Warfare

The Word of God emphatically presents the reality of this world in the beautiful incident of Elijah and Elisha at the time Elijah knew he was to depart this life. Scripture says,

> Now when the Lord was about to take Elijah up to heaven by a whirlwind, Elijah and Elisha were on their way from Gilgal. And Elijah said to Elisha, "Tarry here, I pray you; for the Lord has sent me as far as Bethel." But Elisha said, "As the Lord lives, and as you yourself live, I will not leave you." (2 Kings 2:1-2).

Elisha was determined to find out God's best for his life. Only God's perfect will for him! Anything less was unacceptable.

So the two men went together to Bethel. The students in the school of evangelism there said to Elisha, "Don't you know that the Lord will take away your master from you today?"

"I know it," Elisha replied. "You just keep quiet."

Again, Elijah said, "Now you stay here, young man. The Lord has sent me to Jericho."

"No, I will stick with you," insisted Elisha.

So they went to Jericho where another group of evangelism students tried to discourage Elisha. And again Elijah told him to stay there because the Lord had sent him to the Jordan River.

"I will not leave you," Elisha said again.

At the Jordan, fifty Bible school students watched as Elijah and Elisha stood by the Jordan. I tell you, Israel was in a desperate situation. There were plenty of Bible schools, but very few men of God with the determination to press forward for full blessing!

It's the same today. There are many people who will talk about difficult topics as long as they can do so within the safety of a group. But where can God find an individual to whom He can entrust a difficult message, a man who will then make that message widely known, undeterred by public opinion?

Elijah was a man like that. Elisha was becoming one. Hence his impatience with the mob mentality of that group of Bible school students. He was passing the "prophet test." He must be able to stand alone, to swim against the tide.

Then Elijah took his mantle, rolled it up, and struck the waters, which then divided so the two men could go across just as the Israelites had passed through the Red Sea. On the other side, Elijah said, "Ask what I shall do for you."

What if Elisha had departed the first time, or even the second time that Elijah had told him to stay behind? He would never have heard that question: "What shall I do for you?" You see what a person could miss by not sticking to his purpose?

In reply, Elisha said, "I pray you, let a double portion of your spirit be upon me."

The usual interpretation of this statement is that Elisha had asked for the inheritance right of the oldest son, according to the rule given in Deuteronomy 21:17. I suppose then you would have to assume he had asked to be recognized as the true successor of Elijah, over against all the other young men in the school of prophets.

But I like to interpret his request for a double portion of Elijah's spirit in another way, one in which I can better identify with Elisha. I can imagine that he said, "Elijah, you are a terrific man. Even naturally, you are a giant in every sense of the word. I am just a poor farmer's son. I don't have that character, that personality, that you have. And you are undoubtedly the leader of Israel. There are plenty of Bible schools, but we don't see new leadership coming from them. It looks as though God is going to call me to leadership. How can I ever stand in your shoes unless the Spirit works overtime to make up for my natural weaknesses in comparison to you as a person?"

Elisha may have had poor theology in asking for a "double portion" of the Spirit, as some commentators assert, but his request shows he was a spiritual man. He knew it is not by might or power, but by the Spirit of God that ministry is performed.

Incidentally, Elisha does not make the mistake so many people make. In mission societies that have been founded by great men, some missionaries think they can be the same sort of spiritual giant as the founder. They *cannot!* God's call to men like Hudson Taylor, C. T. Studd, or Cameron Townsend is unique. You cannot duplicate a man who has been given special qualities from God to be the leader in a great pioneer job.

There is a way, however, . . . if . . . IF . . . if only God would give you twice as much of the Holy Spirit as that pioneer had, then you could do the job. That is what Elisha had been thinking for a long time. That's why he didn't want to let go of his master. So now he expresses his strong, passionate desire that twice as much Spirit be upon him as was upon Elijah.

Then the elder prophet replied: "You have asked a hard thing. Nevertheless, if (and that is a big if, an important if) you see the invisible world—if you see me when I am taken from you—then it shall be unto you. If not, it shall not be so."

God is not going to waste the fullness of His Holy Spirit on a person who is too undecided and uncommitted to use it to the full. This principle emphasizes the importance of preparation. Don't think you can just sit at home and skip all training, all discipline and prayer because you suppose the fullness of the Holy Spirit is going to make up for all that. You won't get the blessing, not even the first part of it. Elisha had been a faithful disciple of Elijah for a long time before he came to this climatic point. He had come to realize, as never before, that the *true nature of the battle is spiritual and can only be fought out on a spiritual level*.

If you and I can see that, then God will give us all we need to conquer the enemy, proclaim Christ, and lead His children. But when we ask Him for the fullness of His Holy Spirit, we must permit all of our talent and all of our training to be put at His disposal.

I wish I could have heard the conversation between those two men! They knew Elijah was going to heaven any minute, but they didn't know how. Then, suddenly, as they walked and talked, a chariot of fire and horses of fire appeared and parted them. Elijah went up by a whirlwind into heaven, and *Elisha saw it!* Glory to God! He saw it happen. He saw heaven's taxi! He saw Elijah shoot up into heaven, just as the disciples later saw Jesus go into heaven.

Elisha saw that which no one else could see: he saw the *invisible* world. To him it became visible. What a tremendous moment! I can well understand his cry, "My father, my father! The chariots of Israel and its horsemen!"

Then Elisha tore his own clothes in two. He did not need them anymore since he now had the mantle that had fallen from Elijah. He went back and stood by the bank of the Jordan where those fifty Bible school students who had seen the earlier miracle stood. With the mantle in his hand, Elisha called out: "Where is the Lord, the God of Elijah?" As he struck the waters with the mantle, they separated as before and he walked over.

He had cried, "Where is the Lord, the God of Elijah?" and God answered that prayer. Thereafter, Elisha never again called on the "God of Elijah," because Elijah's God had become his God. If the mantle is on you, if the anointing is on you, if the Spirit is on you, then He is your God. You can do all the things the other saints have done.

What a tremendous story! Authority from the unseen spiritual realm came to a man through his insight into reality and his fellowship with a prophet who walked in the power of God's Spirit. And the authority given to him as a result was manifest to all.

That was a terrific start for Elisha's ministry. And it wasn't a one-time fluke or extraordinary manifestation that wouldn't happen again, because in 2 Kings 6 we see Elisha still living in the power of the Spirit. Elisha and his servant were in the city of Dothan, besieged by a large army with many thousands of soldiers. Elisha's servant despaired as he looked upon the huge host of horses and chariots surrounding the city. "Alas, my master! What shall we do?" he asked.

Surely there are many people today who can sympathize with this man as they look out on the overwhelming forces that seem to be tightening the net around their lives.

But Elisha answered: "Fear not, for those who are with us are more than those who are with them" (v. 16). That sounds a lot like 1 John 4:4: "He who is in you is greater than he who is in the world." Despite what circumstances will tell you, that's the truth. Never forget it!

Then Elisha prayed. I like to put his prayer in my own words: "Lord, I pray you will open his eyes that he may see for a split second what I always see, day and night."

God answered Elisha's prayer: He opened the young man's eyes to see that the mountain was full of horses and chariots of fire around Elisha. For just that moment, because Elisha prayed, his servant saw the invisible world, which exists most of the time out of sight. Such an experience was not the servant's daily portion. It was not his life, not his walk in the

Lord, but for a moment he saw what Elisha was always very much aware of—the invisible world of God's dominion all around him. He saw the angels which, according to Hebrews 1:14, are ministering spirits sent out on behalf of those who inherit eternal life. This is the experience of men and women of God who have been used mightily by God.

We really must include Moses in this discussion. After he had studied all the science and culture of Egypt for forty years, he spent the next forty years tending sheep. He led his flocks to a remote part of the desert near Horeb, the mountain of God. "And the angel of the Lord appeared to him in a flame of fire out of the midst of a bush; and he looked, and lo, the bush was burning, yet it was not consumed" (Ex. 3:2).

This was Moses' first recorded contact with unseen spiritual realities—and it was about time. He was almost 80 years old! In spite of the experience, he was afraid to accept God's commision. He did all he could to persuade God to give it to someone else. Like many in the Christian church today who say, "Lord, here am I, send my sister," so Moses said, "Send my brother. Send Aaron." He did all he could to get away from the call of God. It's pathetic to see what had happened to that once brash man after forty years of desert living.

It would be doing Moses a real injustice, however, to pass lightly over that scene. The martyr Stephen, in his sermon in Acts 7, notes the significant fact that when Moses saw the burning bush "he drew near to look" (v. 31). While Moses at times demonstrated fear of men, he was not afraid of the invisible world; he did not run away when the Lord spoke to him out of the bush.

People are so frightened of the reality of the spiritual world that every time angels appear in the Bible, they have to begin their message with the words, "Fear not." Apparently, people are afraid when the invisible world breaks through into the visible. Moses saw that burning bush and came close. Do we have an appetite, a longing, for the invisible world? Are we willing to press on for a full view?

Moses' life is filled with illustrations of spiritual truth. Another instructive incident is recorded in Numbers 14. There, Moses confronted all of Israel because of a difference in its people's understanding of what was involved in spiritual warfare. After the first spy trip into the Promised Land, the majority of the spies gave their report based on what their physical eyes told them. They were very problem-conscious, and they came back with a negative report. But Caleb and Joshua saw with spiritual eyes; they saw what God could do. They believed in the supernatural, and they saw the potential of the land—if only the people of Israel would move on with God. They remembered that God had told them to "spy out the land of Canaan, which I give to the people of Israel." (Num. 13:2).

Because of God's promise that He would *give* the land to Israel, they made a profession of faith. But the majority of the spies either did not remember the Word of God, or perhaps they remembered it but felt "we still have to conquer it."

Joshua and Caleb's response of faith was indicated by what they said to the people. "Only, do not rebel against the Lord; and do not fear the people of the land, for they are bread for us; their protection is removed from them, and the Lord is with us; do not fear them" (Num. 14:9). Note particularly one aspect of this very wonderful verse. Those heathen nations were said to have had protection! The devil can protect a nation, a group of people, or even individuals so that the Word of God cannot get through to them.

A good illustration of this is the Muslim world. The Muslim world is the only bloc of people in the world who have not yet been penetrated effectively by the Gospel. They are strongly in the grip of a false prophet, because no false religion comes so close to the biblical concept of the kingdom of God as does

Islam. Their holy book, the *Koran,* has many of the stories found in the Bible. Jesus Christ is mentioned often and is counted among the main prophets of the Muslims, but as inferior to Mohammed.

I see a demonic form of protection around the Muslim world, and we Christians have not realized the nature of the spiritual battle and the amount of prayer and sacrifice that will be needed to break through that devilish protection. Don't forget that until 1945, seven-eighths of the Muslim world was under the control of so-called Christian nations. But colonial governments did not encourage gospel preaching because they did not want to antagonize their subjects. They only wanted to exploit them. Now the Arabs can return the favor and exploit our appetite for their oil.

The moment that the oil crisis began in 1977, God gave me a vision of an opportunity. I never complained about higher oil prices because I saw that billions of dollars would now flow into Muslim countries. The money would have to be spent somewhere; it couldn't possibly be spent in those non-industrialized and food-short countries where the greatest amount of oil is generally found. It would have to be spent in the Western world. These oil producers would have to buy technology from us, and that technology would have to be accompanied by westerners who would come as technicians. I could see strategic opportunities arising because now Christians, indeed, are going in as specialists and teachers to reach Muslims not only with technical knowledge, but also with the love of God.

Let me turn now to another example of demonic "protection" that keeps people away from the gospel. When I was in Indonesia a few years ago, I got a copy of the autobiography of Sukarno, president of the country from 1945 to 1967. As a Dutchman, it was very interesting for me to be there because the Dutch did not always treat Sukarno very kindly. He was a revolutionary all his life, and the Dutch imprisoned him and deported him to New Guinea. When he saw his chance, he took it, of course, and fought the Dutch. As a Dutchman, I was there fighting against him at one time.

As I read Sukarno's autobiography, I understood more of the invisible battle. Here are some of his own reflections:

Friends complain that my speeches lately are peppered with references to the time when I shall eventually leave them. Consciously or unconsciously I am readying them and myself for that certain moment when every human being will be called into the presence of the Almighty. I believe strongly in the hereafter. I also believe there are invisible angels near me at all times. The angel at my right does the good deeds. When comes the Day of Reckoning, he'll brag: "Here, Sukarno, are all of your good deeds. Look at them." Then the angel on the left will gloat: "Aaaahhh, Pak, but your vices and dread sins, you will note, make it a much longer list. That being the case I'm afraid we have no choice but to send you to Hell...." I very much fear that if there is really a Doorkeeper in The House of the Lord and he's going to have the say where I go, then...alas...I shall probably plunge straight to Hell. I don't dare hope where He will send me. I hope only that when my time comes, it will be over quickly.[1]

I was deeply struck when I read this. Here was a man who had been hailed by many, almost worshiped by his people when he was in power, and dropped by nearly everyone when he fell from authority. He knew how to express his fear of death so clearly. I could have wept.

"Now there you are, Andrew," I thought to myself, "fighting against such a man. You're just helping him on his way to hell. What are you going to do for him?"

I prayed about the strong urge I had: a deep longing to see Sukarno and to pray with him. So I traveled to Djakarta, the capital city of Indonesia, to see him. He was by then slipping from power and was closely guarded by the military.

"Could I see the general in charge?" I asked.

Strangely enough, they just let me in. The commanding general received me straightaway. "What can I do for you, sir?" he asked.

"I want to see Sukarno."

"Why?"

"I have read his autobiography and have seen on the last pages that he is afraid to die. I want to speak with him about Jesus. I want to pray with him so that when he dies, he can go to heaven."

The general, who was a Muslim, looked at me. He had never heard anything like that before! His response was unusual: "I much appreciate your concern for Sukarno, but this is not the time to think of the life of one man. This is a time to think of the life of a whole nation."

I thought I had heard that before! That sounded like John 11:50 where Caiaphas said it was better for one man to die than for the whole nation to perish.

I pleaded with the general, but no matter what I said, he would not allow me to see Sukarno. They kept him like a prisoner in his palace in Bogor. They didn't want me to even talk publicly about my desire to see him because if I did, the general promised, they would have to throw me out of the country.

"Well," I said, "I haven't talked to anybody, except the Lord."

At that, he mellowed. As we had another cup of coffee, I had the opportunity for almost an hour to preach the gospel to him. I thought, "If I can't get through to Sukarno, then you'll hear the gospel." It was remarkable how open this man was as I spoke about Jesus.

"Later," he promised me, "after the elections, you may try again. You can apply for a visa from his nephew, our ambassador in Bonn, Germany. Then maybe we can let you in."

Later, though, while I was away from Indonesia, I read in the papers that Sukarno had died. I feel he went to a Christ-less grave, even though he certainly knew the way of salvation. I base that belief on the fact that a good friend of mine, a rear admiral of the Indonesian fleet and a fine Christian, had often preached the gospel to Sukarno.

This man entertained many foreign guests, including heads of state from numerous Communist countries. Whenever they were having a meal, the admiral always insisted on saying a prayer. Many people in Indonesia have heard the gospel through such faithful acts as that. It is my hope that some other believer was able to see Sukarno after he wrote his comments about death.

Although Sukarno expressed a firm belief in the invisible world, I am appalled at the lack of conviction of many Christians with regard to this. They are just like the Sadducees in the New Testament who did not believe in angels or in the resurrection.

If, on the other hand, we do believe in the invisible world, if we believe in angels, then no borders are closed, no doors barred! The key to an understanding of what is going on in the world today is just that. It is not communism versus capitalism, but the prince of the power of the air, the prince of darkness, against the Lord Jesus Christ, who is the Prince of Glory and the Savior of the world! Unless we see that our real battle lies in the realm of invisible spiritual forces, we will never take the opportunity to act against hostile governments—even when that is exactly what God wants us to do!

In principle, all earthly authority derives from God under His sovereign will. In practice, however, most earthly authority has sold out to Satan and exists as the visible expression of his demonic force in the invisible world. God's angels are working in that invisible world on behalf of God's servants, but we must never forget that the fiends of hell are desperately active too. In the plan of God, although rulers are meant to be His agents for good, they often defy His will. In reality, many of them are the devil's agents for wrong and evil.

Spiritual warfare of this type goes on now, great powers are locked in a struggle with the world as the prize. That is true politically, economically, militarily, and racially.

But if we accept that the struggle is a spiritual one, then we can believe that it matters what we know and do. Satan would like us to believe that the battle will be decided by armies and governments, by generals and diplomats. But that is not true. The battle will be won by prayer, intercession, and the commitment of Christians all around the world to do God's will.

Theologian Francis Schaeffer emphasizes this when he notes that "our culture, society, government, and law are in the conditions they are in, *not because of a conspiracy, but because the church has forsaken its duty to be the salt of the culture.*"[2] *You* can make a difference! Absurd as it sounds, it is nevertheless true. If the battle is a spiritual one, if the solutions are spiritual ones, then *you*, individually, right from where you live, can make a difference in the battle for the world!

We must not be fatalistic. We *must* believe that individual Christians can intervene in the course of world events and change the course of history. What happens is determined not by some kind of predetermined, inevitable fate. What happens is determined by *our* faith, *our* actions, *our* willingness to take up spiritual burdens and bear them before the Lord.

We must not be spectators in the battle! We can be involved as surely as any diplomat or statesman, as powerfully as any soldier, in the outcome. We can stand by and watch the world collapse before the onslaught of the revolution, or we can find out what is going on and get serious with God about how we can help.

That's what this book is all about.

9
Action Triggers Miracles

Revolution thrives on the failure of the church, and some have said that the rising wave of revolution will cause the church to fall. Actually, the reverse is true. Materialistic revolution succeeds *because* of the failure of the church. Whenever the church fails, such a revolution must gain power.

They are two sides of a coin. If the church does not satisfy the spiritual hunger of people, the poison of the revolution will inevitably flow into the vacuum. The great Russian writer, Alexander Solzhenitsyn, when referring to the Bolshevik Revolution of 1917, has said: "The truth requires me to state that the condition of the Russian Church at the beginning of the twentieth century *is one of the principal causes for the inevitability of the Revolutionary events."*[1]

I have been in the Kremlin Museum in Moscow and have seen a hint of what he was talking about. Displayed there is a huge Bible used by the czars. It is covered with gold, with the diamonds and jewels on the lid so heavy it can hardly be opened with one hand. The robes of the patriarchs, the historical leaders of the Orthodox church, were embroidered with approximately forty-four pounds of gold and silver thread.

All this wealth came from the poor peasant people who were lucky if they had bread to eat. The church in Russia fed on their people's generosity but never gave them the gospel of love in return. The church left the streets and retired to the cathedrals. It became an arm of the establishment, rather than an evangelistic force with a cup of cool water for the needy and the gospel of salvation for the lost. So the revolution came to Russia.

In a different way, the church has also fallen short on many mission fields. Thus, in spite of the missionaries' efforts, the revolution is also on their doorstep too. We have often Christianized people without giving them a first-person faith. And too many missions have responded to the physical suffering of the people and stopped there. To feed the hungry, educate the ignorant, and doctor the sick is good—but if we do all that for people and do not present to them the message of a Jesus who can make them born-again creatures, we have failed. We have ministered to the body only, when the soul, too, was sick. If we have only produced a healthier, better-educated person, whose heart is still empty, he will find something in the passionate ideology of the revolution to fill that empty heart.

The Communists understand this principle better than we do. They have not planted orphanages in Third World countries, as the church has done. They are after the minds of the people and that is the constant focus of their work. Forget about poverty and disease and human misery, they say; better such misery in order to give people something to hate. Then they will become revolutionaries who will ignore every privation in striving for victory.

We, in contrast, need to spend our time giving him someone to love, and someone who loves him—then join hands with him to help him solve his other problems. That seems to be giving a simple solution to complex world problems. But as we enter into spiritual warfare, we discover things happening that we cannot explain. Miracles do happen which show that God is changing the world His way. We are gaining victories that may be known to us only when we get to heaven. So for now, don't try to keep score on how the battle's going, just get involved. Begin to act, and I guarantee you will begin to see miracles happen.

One Sunday, just before I was leaving on a trip to East Germany, I spoke at a large church in Holland and asked intercession for my journey. After the meeting, a slightly agitated lady approached me.

"Andrew, I know you are going to Germany," she said. "Now I have a matter that has been weighing on my conscience. I wish you could help me."

I was puzzled. "Tell me about it," I said.

Obviously under deep conviction of sin, she told me her story.

During, and just after World War II, she lived in the eastern part of Holland near the German border, and used to entertain American officers there in her home. They would often bring textiles to her home. Such cloth was very valuable and especially hard to get in Holland at that time. Because she suspected the officers had stolen it, and also because it was such expensive material, the kind used to make men's suits and linings, she kept it stored away.

The supply increased until she had quite a big box full, but she never used it. Then, for more than twenty years following the war, she worried about it, wondering what to do with it. On that Sunday morning when I spoke in her church, the Lord got through to her and she decided to resolve her problem once and for all.

"Andrew," she asked, "can you please take this to Germany and just give it to someone? It will relieve my conscience to know that to the best of my knowledge it has gone back to where it came from."

I told her I would do that. The next weekend, I loaded my station wagon with all the things I wanted to take across the border. Then, without thinking it over further, I simply put in the big box of cloth she had delivered to me.

When I came to the West German border, an officer asked, "Do you have anything to declare, sir?"

That cloth had great value, but since I was in Germany, I replied, "No, sir," because the cloth had originally come from there and should not need to be declared.

The next morning I arrived at the East German border. Again, that same question from the guard: "Do you have anything to declare?"

"Yes," I answered. "A lot!"

I opened the rear of my station wagon. "Here," I said, "is a box full of cloth that I want to take into the country."

"What are you going to do with it?" he asked.

"I will give it away."

"To whom?"

"I don't know."

Well, that really brought the question marks to his face! So I added, "I can explain it to you, sir."

I gave him the story of what had happened the previous Sunday morning, but I extended it a little so that it became a full-fledged sermon on restitution and the need for a clean heart. I also put in something about God's forgiveness being available to all men. Of course, I used the story of the lady, but I made it just a little longer to get the gospel across to the officer at the border.

All this time, he had a deeply puzzled look on his face. He turned to me. "Sir," he said, "I'll have to talk it over with my bosses inside the office. I have never had a case like this before."

He went inside and twenty minutes passed before he came out again. He had talked to all his superiors in the office and had still come up with no answer.

"Tell me again," he inquired, "to whom are you going to give it?"

"Honestly," I said, "I don't care." Then I asked, "Do you want it?"

"Oh, no, I can't take it."

"Well, all right, I just want to give it to somebody."

"Where?"

"I don't know," I said. "I want to give it back to somebody in Germany. I am going to be traveling all over the country. Listen, if you don't know what to do and I can't pass with all of this, you may seal it; and I'll just take it into West Berlin and give it away to someone there. But this lady did receive it from Germany, and she wants me to give it to someone in Germany. That's all."

Again, he had that deeply perplexed look. He went back into the office and phoned, probably all the way to East Berlin. He didn't know what to do. After a long, long time, he came out to me again and just shrugged his shoulders. "Sir, just take it, go, and give it to anybody you want."

He never asked me if I had anything *else* to declare, but I had told him the truth when he asked if there was any *thing* to declare. I had truthfully shown him one box of cloth that had to be declared. He became nonplussed by my lengthy explanation, but maybe something I said may have been used by God to work in his heart anyway.

So he let me pass. They had never had such a case before. Usually, if you have so much as a dollar's worth of goods you have to declare it. I had hundreds of dollars' worth and no written declaration, and he let me take it in to give it away to whomever I chose.

I call that a miracle!

Later in the afternoon, I drove into the city where I would spend the night and went to the home of a tailor with whom I usually stayed. There I found a young Hungarian lady named Anna. She was the daughter of a Baptist pastor who had served as my interpreter in Hungary. I had put the two families, one in East Germany and the other in Hungary, in touch with each other.

"What are you doing here, Anna?" I asked in surprise.

"As you know," Anna explained, "my parents are very poor. So my mother has sent me to East Germany to find some cloth to make a suit for Daddy."

Well, I thought I was in heaven! Such clear guidance! I had worked a great deal with her father, who ministered among Gypsies in Hungary. He was a real man of God, thrown out of the ministry because he distributed Bibles to the troops of the Russian army. His lack of a regular occupation brought great poverty to the family.

Because I was in the house of a tailor, I could cut off just enough of the cloth for this man's suit, and the rest I could still give away to other people who needed it.

Now every little detail was in place, truth prevailing and God's power so evident. Guidance given to everyone involved—the woman in Holland, the border guards in East Germany, the tailor, and the fine Baptist pastor in Hungary! And to think this girl arrived at this very time on the opposite side of the very same errand that had brought me to this home. It was marvelous!

I want to emphasize yet another principle of spiritual warfare that the Lord Jesus has called us to wage in His name. Because He holds all authority in heaven and on earth, and because His hosts surround us with their power in the invisible world, we who are obedient to Him can expect that our Almighty God will bring His purposes to pass through nothing less than miracles.

What is a miracle? A miracle is the sovereign act of God

based on Truth. The Truth! Truth on my part, of course, in the conviction that God *is* the Truth.

Nor are there any small miracles. Every miracle is big, whether you get a penny when you need a penny or a million dollars when you need that. The miracle is equally wonderful in both cases. And such things don't happen only at the border, but anywhere and anytime for anyone who is faithful in the Lord's service.

I tell people that if I take Bibles across a border once and something remarkable happens, you might call it a coincidence. But if I did that full-time for over twenty years (as I have), and that now we have scores of teams doing it each year and nearly always something happens to distract the guards' attention, then you could not possibly call all of those happenings coincidence. It's God's miraculous guidance and intervention!

But God is not a prankster who does wonderful things just to show off His power. Every miracle of God occurs for the purpose of advancing the cause of Jesus Christ and for bearing witness to the gospel, directly or indirectly.

On one occasion early in my ministry, I was headed back home from Berlin through the one hundred mile Russian-occupied zone of East Germany. I had been working in the refugee camps with a fellow Dutchman named Anton, giving out Scriptures to people from different countries. We had some Bibles left over which I was taking back with me to Holland where I could repack them and send them with other teams to the specific Eastern European countries that could use them.

I had not hidden the Bibles; I just had them in cardboard boxes. So far I had never encountered any problems going through the East German border into West Germany. This time though, as I stopped at Helmstadt, on the East German side of the border, an officer came up to my car and pointed to one of the cardboard boxes. "What's in there?" he asked.

With a very big smile, I said, "Sir, there are Bibles in that box."

He frowned. "Take the box into my office," he ordered.

So Anton and I carried the heavy box into his office and filled three tables with New Testaments, Gospels, and complete Bibles, mostly in Eastern European languages.

He checked every book to see where it had been printed. I was lucky none had been printed in New York, since anything printed in America would have been more suspect. But they were all from Sweden, Germany, Switzerland, and Holland.

"Do you have anything else?" he asked.

Again I smiled, and said, "Yes, sir, I have a lot more."

He marched us back to our vehicle, right to the back of my Volkswagen and pointed to a box. "What's in there?"

"Flannelgraph stories."

"What's that?"

I have developed a habit of making very long sentences, so I can present the gospel at every opportunity. I launched in.

"Well, sir," I responded, "they are illustrated stories that teachers use to tell children about the Lord Jesus Christ, because even children can believe on Him; because when a child is old enough to love his parents, he can love Jesus who came into the world to save sinners so that children as well as grown-up people, by simple faith in Him, can have eternal life and go to heaven when they die."

That was my sermonette in a sentence!

He left the box right there, but then he pulled out one of the folders and opened it. I was embarrassed because it was a map of the Mediterranean with the travels of the apostle Paul marked with dots and lines, all the countries, seas, and islands identified. It looked like a proper spy map!

Looking at me very closely, he said, "Aha! You said it was for little children—"

"Yes, sir," I interrupted, "it's just a map of the travels of the apostle Paul, the first to come to Europe to tell about the Lord Jesus Christ so that we in Europe should hear about the great message of Jesus Christ; and if Paul had not come here, we would still be barbarians living without God—practically as atheists."

That was my second sermonette!

He really got cross with me then. "Take that box into my office!"

We saw that the office was full of soldiers, picking up those beautiful books we had laid out on the tables, trying to read the Word of God in these different languages. When I put the box down, more people flowed into the hall, Red Army soldiers and officers.

The officer pulled another folder from my box and, again, it was the worst possible one he could have chosen. It was the story of Ephesians 6, the chapter on the whole armor of God! When he opened it, out fell the sword and the helmet and all the rest. The situation looked dangerous to me.

Again an angry look appeared on his face as he mumbled something more about "children."

"Really, it is!" I insisted. "Let me demonstrate it for you"

I asked my friend Anton, who is six-and-a-half-feet tall, to hold up the cloth background. I took a figure of an undressed boy and stuck it to the flannel background, and began to tell the story.

"Here is a man in the world, unprotected from sin and demons, and sickness, and darkness, and disease. He needs protection. Man cannot live without God..."

I put on him the helmet of salvation.

"You've got to believe in the Lord Jesus Christ to be saved and know that you have eternal life."

Then I quickly put on the breastplate of righteousness.

"...because you have to live a righteous life, and all these godless people in this world make a mess of it and murder people..." I gave the story of Hitler's Germany. "...and now we can't allow that to happen because people living without God bring the whole world into bondage."

Then I put the shield of faith in the little figure's hand and said that with faith we are protected. "No matter what happens in the world, if we have personal faith which results in a new heart, we can live a holy life and have the shield of faith, so that all the onslaughts of the enemy, all his attacks, can be thwarted right here with the shield of faith."

I was just going to grab the sword and put it on the flannel board and go on to speak about the Word of God, when it dawned on the officer that I was preaching to them! I surely had a captive audience; the office was filled with soldiers and officers!

"Now, stop this! Put it all back in your boxes and take it to your car and go!"

"Yes, sir," I said. "But I would first like to give each of you a souvenir. I've enjoyed my time with you."

I got out a pile of John's Gospels and tried to hand them out, but the soldiers couldn't possibly accept them. They put their hands behind their backs and marched away, leaving Anton and me to take the Bibles and flannelgraph stories back to the car.

A hundred yards up the road we were stopped by traffic police for speeding! In my enthusiasm I had not noticed there was a speed limit of three miles an hour. I really didn't think it fair that I had to pay a fine after such a good opportunity for preaching!

This incident illustrates the point that with God working miracles, we don't have to outsmart the guards at border crossings. But we do have to go prepared in prayer, assured that we are in God's will. If I have my car loaded with Bibles as I arrive at the Russian border, I just beam at the guards. I have already prayed hard before I left that they won't ask, "Do you have any Bibles?" Sometimes I pray something will distract their thoughts and attention. It is remarkable how the Lord just arranges for "little" things to happen at the border.

For example, one of our teams went to Bulgaria with a load of Bibles in a huge pick-up van. Since it was summer and we travel just like other tourists—which we are in a way because we enjoy the sunshine and scenery, the swimming and all the rest—the two fellows had an inflatable canoe with them for recreation. They had been lazy that day and after canoeing somewhere in Yugoslavia, they didn't bother to let the air out of the canoe. They just squeezed the whole thing into the back end of the van and drove off to the Bulgarian border with their seven hundred Bibles.

At the border they gave their papers to one of the officers while another officer, blissfully innocent, went to the rear of the van and opened the door.

Bang! The canoe shot out the door right onto his head! He stood there for a moment, completely befuddled. Our boys were helpful; they ran to him, lifted the canoe off his head, and together they pushed it back into the car, locked the door, and that was the end of the inspection. You could never arrange for that to happen a second time.

Another team went to Czechoslovakia with Bibles. Just before they reached the border, they stopped for a last prayer meeting before crossing. Being Dutch boys, they made themselves a cup of coffee and opened a tin of milk. But, also because they were boys, they forgot to put it away properly, leaving the open tin on a box partly filled with Bibles, partly with tools.

While they were in the office at the border-crossing having their papers checked, one of the officers opened the van to check the luggage. Somehow he knocked over that tin of milk and spilled some on the floor. He jumped out of the vehicle and ran to his office, got a cloth and ran back and began to wipe up the spilled milk. He apologized profusely and was ever so sorry—and there was no more checking whatsoever! A tin of milk did that. It's often something small like that that God uses in a big way.

Not long ago, I was returning from a trip in the East and stayed overnight in Germany. Contrary to my usual practice, I had taken my papers out and put them in a drawer in the desk of my room at the hotel. When I left the place, I forgot all about my papers in the drawer. I didn't discover they were missing until I was very close to the Dutch border.

What was I to do? As a foreigner you might get into Holland without showing your passport, but as a Dutchman you cannot. It is absolutely impossible. Every Dutchman has to show his papers—car papers and passport—at the border-crossing. I have never seen anybody get across without them.

I waited there in line behind the other cars, with my window open to the nice weather. Everybody was showing papers, and it went very quickly. There was the customs officer, and maybe just six feet away, a painter was working, restriping the bar that normally stops traffic. My turn came next.

I leaned out of the window and began saying the first two words of my explanation to the official: "I haven't—" when just then the painter said something funny to the customs officer, and he turned to the painter and waved me through with his hand!

No problem. I'm sure I was the only Dutchman that day, or that week, or that month, who got through without showing papers. And it happened the very second I needed it. That was the Lord's working! If it had not happened, I could have spent a lot of time trying to get through.

When I got home, again no problem. I phoned the hotel and

they sent my documents by registered mail. The Lord often does that. For those people who feel that living and working this way is not for them, I just say: "Well, then, it means that the Lord is not calling you to do this kind of work." I think that should settle it.

I hope no one makes the mistake of concluding, in view of these incidents I've described, that this is an easy business. I cannot tell you how many times I have devoted myself to prayer and fasting to prove to myself that I am willing to pay the price. While it is wonderfully true that our victory has been assured in the Lord Jesus, we can never forget that the territory which we are commanded to invade is truly occupied right now by the enemy of Christ. I don't mind confessing that my knees tremble sometimes—but that doesn't make my faith waver.

10
The Truth, the Whole Truth

I have often stated that I am determined not to tell a lie, but I often pray mighty hard that I won't have to tell the truth either. That may sound like a paradox, but it isn't the contradiction it may seem.

The real problem for us may be that living under liberty we have forgotten that the people of God have almost always been a desperate, destitute minority. Compare them with liberation movements, dissidents, underground resistance fighters, you name it. God's people have always had to make some sort of accommodation with regard to how far they would go in telling "the truth, the whole truth, and nothing but the truth."

Someone might say, "But look at Daniel. He didn't sneak around; he lived triumphantly under three foreign, anti-God rulers! He didn't have to compromise!" Sounds great, but ...the people of God are more in the class of Daniel's three friends who were thrown into the fiery furnace. Their situation has pretty well remained the position of the church throughout the centuries. These are the ones with whom God identifies, and hence He is known to them as:

- "A defense for the helpless."
- "A defense for the needy in distress."
- "A refuge from the storm."
- "A shade from the heat."

He is the God "who will wipe away tears from all faces," the one who will remove "the reproach of his people from all the earth" (Is. 25:4, 8). The people who have identified with God have had to run for their lives, even though they were God-anointed and God-appointed! David had to run for his life because of a conspiracy (2 Sam. 15–18). But David not only organized confusion in his enemy's camp, he also prayed against his conspirators (2 Sam. 15:31), which is another lesson of spiritual battle we need to learn. But we cannot use these and other stories of the Bible in an unrelated way as our code of conduct, a very unspiritual use of the Holy Scriptures. By inclination we too often choose those that support a non-confrontive position. Confrontation cannot always be avoided.

Now there are several ways I come at this matter of handling the truth when dealing with the enemy. Remember, we who love the Lord are in the service of the truth, and we know that truth is the basis on which God works His miracles. So I want to stress again what I have said before: I do not lie.

But, at the same time, I believe we can ethically conceal the whole truth. That is, we do not always have to reveal everything we know about a situation. Here's an illustration of how that works.

One Sunday morning, a Christian boy was going to one of the secret house meetings of believers behind the Iron Curtain. Everyone knew that the police were trying to find out where the church was meeting, so his father warned him to be careful to watch out for the police.

All alone, the boy made his way quietly toward the meeting house. Christians have to go to these meetings one at a time in order not to attract attention to what is going on. Other members of the family have to go at different times and take different routes to the meeting place. I have done this myself.

Walking along rapidly, this boy was suddenly stopped by a

policeman who had been hiding behind a tree. "Stop!" he ordered. "Where are you going?"

The boy stood there for a moment, determined not to tell a lie, but probably equally determined not to tell the truth. He must have shot a telegram prayer to heaven, for he looked the policeman in the eye and with a very sad face he said: "Sir, I am going to see my brothers and sisters. This morning we are going to open the testament of my oldest brother."

The policeman assumed he meant his older brother had died and that the family was gathering for the reading of his last will and testament. So he took pity on him and said, "All right Sonny, on you go!"

The boy's reply saved the situation for the church. He had not told a lie, but had told the truth in a way that concealed the whole truth. The boy had clearly (to a believer) said he was going to meet with his brothers and sisters in Christ in order to study the Word of God, but he said it the way he did because he knew he was dealing with an enemy who was not entitled to know the truth.

Biblical ethics regarding how to carry on spiritual warfare and remain truthful cannot stay on the level of theory but must deal with specific actions. Our strategy is often designed to deceive the enemy, to make him think one thing is intended, when actually something else is happening.

In the work we do in restricted countries, we believe we do not have to tell our enemy all of our moves. We do inform our prayer partners around the world about some of our program; but as to the details of strategy, we can't even tell our close prayer partners everything. We cannot risk putting our contacts in danger, and we are even far less likely to make public our strategy, and thus give it to our opposition.

It's a principle of strategy to take actions which deceive or confuse the enemy; lying is not necessarily involved. Joshua 8 offers a helpful example of what I mean.

The Truth, the Whole Truth

The Hebrews were expecting to conquer Ai, the second city in Canaan, as easily as they had just captured Jericho. But something went wrong. Because there was a traitor in the camp, a man who put his personal interests ahead of his nation's interest, they lost the first battle and many lives. That situation of sin in the camp had to be corrected.

We read: "The Lord said to Joshua, 'Stretch out the javelin that is in your hand toward Ai; for I will give it unto your hand' " (Josh. 8:18). But this time Joshua's battle plan was to be different. Before, he had been told to lie in ambush in order to conquer the city, this time he was to retreat, in what might be called a "simulated defeat."

Joshua was under no obligation, of course, to inform the enemy that the retreat he made was not for real. It was just a maneuver to get the enemy out of the city so that the other army which he had hidden could come in and set fire to the city. The ensuing panic resulted in the complete destruction of the e emy's army. Joshua didn't have to reveal that to the captains of Ai before starting his fake retreat. This was strategy for war! The people of Ai failed to see through Joshua's plan and were taken in by his maneuver.

Truth is always the basis upon which the Lord works miracles in answer to believing prayers, but it is often truth *concealed* as far as the understanding of the enemy is concerned. According to Mark 4:11–12, this is the reason Jesus taught in parables, to conceal truth from some eyes. This factor becomes one of the Christian's best weapons against the enemy who remains incapable of understanding the ways of God and truth. We can use the truth in many ways without telling our enemy what he has no right or business to know.

Again in the Old Testament we find an incident in the life of one of the greatest men of God, the prophet Samuel, to prove our point. He had anointed Saul to be king; then Saul proved unworthy of this great honor and God rejected him. Samuel grieved over this, but the Lord said to him: "How long will you grieve over Saul, seeing I have rejected him from being king over Israel? Fill your horn with oil, and go; I will send you to Jesse the Bethlehemite, for I have provided for myself a king among his sons" (1 Sam. 16:1).

God gave Samuel a clear command in order to preserve Israel as a nation. This command would maintain the line from which the Messiah would be born. Now David, a man after God's heart, would be in the line of His Son.

But Samuel was afraid (v. 2). "How can I go? If Saul hears it, he will kill me." Apparently, the people were already living in a police state, under a dictatorship. The situation had gone that far. The devil was attempting to use this man Saul, who previously had been anointed of God, to destroy the line of the Messiah. By doing this, Satan thought he could make it impossible for the kingdom of God to break through in this world.

You may want to study this line of thought for yourself; God's work of preservation is written throughout the whole of Scripture. Whether in the tribulations of Joseph, or of the Israelites in Egypt, or other salient incidents in the Old Testament, they are all part of the strategy of Satan to eliminate the possibility of Jesus ever being born in Bethlehem of Judea.

"If Saul hears it, he will kill me." Samuel was afraid.

The Lord then said to Samuel, "Take a heifer with you." A heifer would suggest that Samuel planned to make a sacrifice, not to anoint a new king.

Now wait a minute, some might exclaim. Is God telling Samuel that he is to hide his real errand? Cover it up? Do something that many people would call unethical? But here the Almighty God Himself instructs Samuel to cover up his actions, to camouflage his purpose, to tell only part of the truth!

In my mind I think God was saying, "Now, listen, Samuel,

this is what you do: you take a heifer with you, and if Saul's police stop you, you just smile at them and say, 'Oh, I'm going to sacrifice to the Lord; just look at this heifer. I am going to Bethlehem, and I am going to invite Jesse to the sacrifice.' "

But God gave in advance the real purpose of the trip: "Samuel, while you do that, I will show you what more you shall do: you shall anoint for me him whom I name to you."

Certainly we seem to have here divine authorization for the concealment of motives. You may call it evasion, or a failure to reveal the whole truth, but the most important fact is there was no untruth in what the Lord authorized. The Lord never asks that. Saul had no right to know the whole purpose of Samuel's mission to Jesse, nor was Samuel under obligation to disclose it. Concealment is not lying. In serving God one must be careful to guard the distinction between veiled or partial truth and untruth.

Remember what we've said: Jesus is the King of Kings, and His orders take priority over all the decrees of human governments, especially when godless men try to restrict or prohibit the spread of the gospel. This is a fact of divine revelation which is not open to argument or rationalization. "We must obey God rather than men" (Acts 5:29). It's simply a matter of priority.

As I have said before, I pray hard that I don't have to tell the truth. But to not tell the truth is not necessarily the same as telling a lie, especially if I am withholding the *whole truth* from people who have utterly forfeited the right to know what I am concealing.

If I am at the border of an unfriendly country and have my car loaded with Scriptures, I am under no obligation whatsoever to tell the border guards all about my motives and my cargo. They are in the service of the devil, and their aim is to prevent the kingdom of God from coming to this world. They will attempt to prevent it, using the most cruel means possible: suppressing the truth, killing pastors, imprisoning believers, and burning churches.

Unfortunately, most of the individuals I confront at the border, the guards and the police, are all a part of that system. Though I love them as people, I don't love their system, which is in the service of the devil himself to stamp out the church so that the kingdom of God will not come to this world.

Jesus, Himself, concealed truth from the Pharisees and leaders who were enemies of God. "And when He was alone, those who were about Him with the twelve asked Him concerning parables. And He said to them, 'To you has been given the secret of the kingdom of God, but for those outside everything is in parables; so that they may indeed see but not perceive, and may indeed hear but not understand" (Mark 4:10–12).

The enemies of God were already sinning against the truth they had. If they were told more truth it would only mean more condemnation. God, in grace, mercy, and love, does not want them to know certain things lest their judgment be made even greater.

At times, some border guards and policemen seem not to want more knowledge of what we are doing for the same reason. They do not want to be responsible for even more rebellion against God and His people.

Jesus showed mercy to King Herod in Luke 23:9, for Herod "questioned Him at some length; but He made no answer." I think His reason for silence is clear, because in the same passage we read how Herod had reviled and mocked Jesus. The king was not ready to hear and act on truth.

I am not advocating the same thing as what is known as situational ethics, which says that a person may do immoral things (for instance, adultery, lying, stealing) if the situation demands it (to save his life or freedom). I don't advocate that at all. I am saying we must always obey God's truth. It never changes, although sinners may change their rules and laws as they battle against God's truth and kingdom. Our hearts' intent and our actions as well must always be truthful, although people committed to Satan's kingdom will accuse us of the opposite, even though they have no claim or right to have more of the truth.

That does not mean that you must hate such persons. We are fighting against their master, and his plans and ideology which has caught them in his error. We should always look for a chance to share with them the saving truth of the gospel of Jesus Christ.

Our Lord commands us to go and proclaim. Defeat the enemy. You are in God's business. So when you come to a border-crossing, at that point the enemy has no right to know what you are doing, if he would use the truth to fight against God's truth. Because the enemy has utterly forfeited the right to know the truth, concealment may be an obligation which the truth itself requires.

In dealing with people when mutual understanding is important, then, and only then, are we under obligation to ensure that truth is not concealed by what we say and do. In their case, you see, they have a claim to the truth.

Consider the Great Commission again. Jesus said, "Go into all the world and preach the gospel..." (Mark 16:15). Note that He didn't say we must first have a conference with the enemy. Jesus Himself did not have a conference with the devil to settle their warfare by common agreement. You cannot have a dialogue with your enemy—not in the realm of the spirit. Jesus had no such dialogue with the devil.

Along with concealment, there is a principle of partial truth that should not be mistaken for untruth. In Exodus 1, the midwives of the Hebrews were ordered to kill all the baby boys born to the Jews (no one demanded that the mothers themselves do it!). The midwives didn't obey the order, so the king of Egypt called the midwives and said, "Why have you done this, and let the male children live?" (v. 18).

The midwives said, "Because the Hebrew women are not like the Egyptian women; for they are vigorous and are delivered *before* the midwife comes to them" (v. 19).

What is this? For one thing, it's speaking the truth. Modern doctors now know that a pregnant woman will have an easier delivery if she keeps moving and does exercises. But if she sits in a chair or lies in bed all those months, her delivery is likely to be more difficult. The Hebrew women in Egypt had to work hard. They were slaves, and they were exploited. It was terrible, but it kept them so healthy and strong that the midwives didn't have much to do. Of course the babies came more quickly than with Egyptian women! But this had been true even before Pharaoh's command, so the midwives, while giving a truthful answer, were not telling all they knew—partial truth.

Just to review another basic principle of spiritual warfare: notice that the midwives disobeyed Pharaoh, the legal authority, because "they feared God" (v. 21). Remember, we either break God's commands and stick to our own man-made, super-pious traditions, or we break our traditions and become vital Christians in the way Jesus and the apostles were. Not fearing Pharaoh, not fearing the enemy, but obeying God— the choice is ours. We can take the biblical advice not to be "frightened [intimidated] in anything by your opponents" (Phil. 1:28).

Another useful employment of the truth is interpretation. While there is no law that Bibles should not be imported into Communist countries, there is a law that you have to declare all the goods you have. I tell you, it can be pretty tricky at times!

I had taken several loads of Scriptures into the Soviet Union and had no trouble. I had not exactly put them on display, and customs checks had never stopped them.

But one day the Russians came up with a new idea at the border. They had a big form for me to fill out. One of the questions was "Are you taking into the Soviet Union any literature, written or printed, that could do damage to the political and economic situation of the Soviet Union?" I was carrying a load of eight hundred Bibles, plus thousands of tracts. I knew that on the other side were hundreds of pastors to whom I'd promised to give a Bible. In my heart, I realized the Bible could, indeed, "damage" the existing political situation in Russia.

I admit I was pinned down at that moment. So I decided to change some money and get my insurance papers ready. I knew I couldn't fill out that form; I couldn't sign because I had Bibles, the very Word of God!

Quietly I prayed: "Lord God, give me light. I want to obey you, only you, no one else. There are people praying for a Bible, and I am going to be the answer to their prayers; yet I am not going to tell a lie. Help me! What can I do?"

I knew I couldn't turn around and go back. If I turned around and went back into Poland, they would probably ask, "Why didn't you go further?"

As I prayed, the Lord gave me an idea. He said: "Andrew, you're not going to sell those Bibles on the black market (they could bring two- or three-hundred dollars each) and become a millionaire overnight, so you are not going to do any damage to the economic situation. You are going to give them to believers. You are not going to give them to Khruschev or Kosygin or Brezhnev or any other Communist party leaders. You are going to give them to pastors who need tools to teach their flocks more of the truth of God's way. So you are not going to do violence to the political situation; it's only for the kingdom of God."

I found peace in my heart. I took my pen and signed the paper. God had given me the interpretation that satisfied my heart. At the same time, I was also ready to accept the risk that the Bibles would be found and the authorities would not agree with the explanation I might give for my declaration. But my God is the same God who identifies with Peter in prison, and with Daniel's friends in the fiery furnace.

Recently I had a deep conversation with one of the great evangelical leaders of our time. We discussed the type of questions that come up: where are those Bibles? Or the one Corrie ten Boom faced: where are those Jews? Or like the Russian believers have to deal with: where is the pastor? Where is the secret Bible printing press?

My friend went much further than I ever had on this subject. He said to me, "Andrew, whenever the enemy comes to you with a question, you have to understand what is behind his question. You must first *interpret* the question before you answer. For instance, if I were in the position of Corrie ten Boom, when the soldiers asked, 'Do you have any Jews in your house?' and I had to decide whether I would tell the truth or not, I would first have to ask myself, 'What is the man asking?' I have to interpret his question. He's asking me, 'Do you have a Jew in this house *that I can arrest and kill?*' Then the complete answer is, 'No, I do not have a Jew in this house that you can arrest and kill.' But I would say to him, simply, 'No.' "

Please note that what I have just described is not my position, but that which was given to me by a very godly man whose judgment I respect. It helps me a great deal in looking back on the history of my own dear Christian friends in Holland who did many illegal things during the Nazi occupation to thwart the forces of evil.

In fact, in a Biblical situation similar to our experience in Holland, God seems to have allowed direct untruths to be used to accomplish His purpose. In Hebrews 11:31, it says: "By faith Rahab the harlot did not perish with those who were disobedient, because she had given friendly welcome to the spies."

Her action was illegal. Her local government was opposed to Israel, and Israel was set on conquering her king, her government, and her people. But she had seen the issue was a spiritual one (Joshua 2), and had chosen in her heart to follow the God of Israel, although as yet she knew very little about Him.

The whole fascinating story began when the soldiers (let's call them police) came to her home and said, "You have entertained men of Israel who have come here to search out the land. Bring them out of your house that we may arrest them. Here is the arrest warrant. Our government wants them."

But the woman had taken the two men and hidden them. Listen carefully now to what she says: "True, men came to me, but I did not know where they came from." Was that the truth? No, it was not. "And when the gate was to be closed at dark, the men went out." Was that the truth? No, it was not. "Where the men went I do not know." Was that the truth? No. "Pursue them quickly, for you will overtake them."

Actually she had taken the spies up to the roof where she hid them in the stalks of flax (v. 6). Then, when the police went to search outside the gate, she took the spies out, got their promise to spare her life and deal kindly with her family, and let them down over the wall, and they escaped.

That's an amazing story. She hides spies, she tells lies, she helps the spies escape.

But look at this story in the way my friend suggested we

should, interpreting the question first before answering. If you listened carefully to the question asked by the Jericho police, the enemy of God's people, it was this: "Have you hidden any people here that we want to arrest and kill before they succeed in establishing the kingdom of God here?"

Obviously, the answer is no. Rahab's reply said, in effect, "I am not on your side; I am on the side of the God of Israel. I cannot assist you in destroying the spies."

A thin line? Yes, but an extremely important one—and indeed one which God has honored when used both by believers *and* unbelievers. I doubt Rahab would have advanced the argument given above. But however she justified her act, Rahab is in God's list of heroes! "By faith, Rahab the harlot did not perish with those who were disobedient, because she had given friendly welcome to the spies" (v. 31).

The Lord doesn't praise her for telling lies. I'm sure He forgave her sin because of her faith. He praises her for her attitude, and her risky and dangerous action. Look at James 2:25: "And in the same way was not also Rahab the harlot justified by works?" It's what she did: her action was a result of her attitude, her disposition, her allegiance.

The truth can be understood also with reference to circumstances of change. When conditions are altered, or your companions or your opponents change, then you consequently have to change behavior, attitude, and sometimes even words that previously seemed appropriate.

Consider what Moses said in essence to Pharaoh: "We just want to make a three-days' journey into the wilderness to sacrifice, and then we will be back" (Ex. 5). He even sets certain limitations on who was going to join him: "not the whole nation but just some."

But Pharaoh cheated on Moses and the situation changed. After the plagues, which came because of Pharaoh's hard heart, he finally did let Moses go—but with *all* the Israelites, their wives, children, cattle, and all their possessions. What had once been a three-day journey, for some, became the exodus of all of the people. The point is that when Moses left Egypt he knew very well he would never be back—and he hadn't promised that to Pharaoh either! Because Pharaoh had, after the months of negotiations, changed his attitude and hardened his heart; there was a change of plans and of behavior in Moses which he didn't care to reveal to Pharaoh! The truth was contigent on circumstantial changes.

Remember the story of Jonah's preaching mission to Nineveh? He told them that because of their sins, God would destroy their city in forty days. But God never did destroy it, because the people met His conditions by repenting. The situation changed because their behavior changed, so God's word changed. God changed His mind.

Just the opposite sequence of events happened in the case of King Saul. God rejected and replaced Saul (whom He had once chosen and anointed as king) because Saul had changed and no longer measured up to God's requirements.

A quite remarkable example of the truth that circumstances make a difference with regard to ethical considerations also appears in the life of our Lord Jesus Himself. In John 7:1 we read: "After this Jesus went about in Galilee; he would not go about in Judea, because the Jews sought to kill him."

Of course it was not all Jews who wanted to kill Him, but only those who craftily manipulated the government. They themselves had no authority to have people executed (John 18:31), although Jesus must have appeared to them and to the government to be a hostile intruder who wanted to establish another kingdom (Luke 23:2). In fact, He did resist the religious, political, and economic systems of His day, just as He throws down the gauntlet to every system not based on truth and righteousness today.

Jesus' explanation of why He could not go to Judea was

"My time has not yet come, but your time is always here" (John 7:6).

In other words, Jesus implied that if you always agree with the local government, then you can always go about freely because you just don't get into trouble. That's one sure way to avoid persecution: always agree with your government—good or bad; "my country, right or wrong."

Then the Lord said: " 'Go to the feast yourselves; I am not going up to this feast, for my time has not yet fully come.' " So saying, He remained in Galilee" (vv. 8–9).

But after His brothers had gone up to this feast, He also went (v. 10)! Not publicly, but in private, or in secret, as other Bible versions have it. He clearly circumvented the wishes of government authorities.

Jesus working in secret? Jesus going underground? Jesus disobeying government orders? Could it be so? If He set this precedent, could not some of His followers do the same? They have been commanded to walk in His footsteps (1 John 2:6).

In John 12:35–36, we are taught the principle on which Jesus' actions were based. " 'The light is with you for a little longer. Walk while you have the light, lest the darkness overtake you; he who walks in the darkness does not know where he goes. While you have the light, believe in the light, that you may become sons of light.' When Jesus had said this, He departed and hid Himself from them."

What did Jesus say? Walk while you have the light. There comes a time when night comes, and then no man can work (John 9:4). By analogy, there also comes a time when we don't have the light or the liberty to go about witnessing for Him. Then, He says, we will have to change our methods. A change in behavior comes in response to a change in circumstances.

Governments may change. Instead of a democratically chosen government, we may get a dictatorship. Then our actions will have to change. The situation demands that we act in accordance with the relevant facts and conditions.

Because the body of believers around the world lives under so many different kinds of governments, the response of Christians in other countries is very different from that of Christians who have only lived in freedom. Our lack of understanding explains why we have sent missionaries only to countries where they are officially accepted. For other situations we have no standard textbooks to go by, no biographies of God's great warriors to turn to for answers and guidance. How they lived and worshiped and witnessed is shrouded in silence because it did not suit their governments to make known their battle for truth.

Throughout this discussion, I have insisted I would not tell a lie. That is a personal conviction, if you will, because I want to see God's miracles on my behalf. But it is evident from the examples given here that revealing something less than all we know is warranted in many circumstances. In any situation in which we might justify any type of civil disobedience because of godless civil authorities, or because of their attempts to limit our witness, then deception through feigned actions is justified. Our obedience has to reflect our loyalty to God rather than to those who would use us to advance the kingdom of Satan.

11
Should We Smuggle Bibles?

At this time in history there are unfortunately more and more governments than ever before that attempt to prohibit the import of the Word of God, whether in printed form, or as a spoken witness by missionaries. Whatever the form the entrance of evangelistic missions take, these governments attempt to close their borders and to defy the command of our King.

Jesus told us we must go into all the world and preach the gospel. Since any specific law in this world must be superseded by whatever higher law exists, I contend that this supreme command, coming from God Himself, is the one I must obey. Even if a lower law tells me I should not do something, I have to break that law in order to keep God's law.

So I take the Bible in anyway; I go to preach anyway. But if I am a lawbreaker, if I am indeed a smuggler, I am guilty only to the same degree that Jesus was in His earthly ministry when He transgressed human rules. In this same sense, Jesus smuggled, and His disciples smuggled.

I have had many discussions on this with people whose sincerity I don't doubt for a moment; they think smuggling Bibles is unethical. They say that if a government forbids the importation of Bibles, then we should obey the government, whether it be Russian or Cuban or Chinese. But, if you reason along that line, it means the apostles should never have gone into any country in Europe. If you study the New Testament, you will see that not a single country ever *invited* the apostles to come in. On the contrary, they were persecuted by the authorities. It was by going into hiding, or doing illegal things as far as governments were concerned, that they succeeded in getting the gospel out.

We must remain under the same imperative today. We must get the gospel across to every person. Whether we send in diplomats, businessmen, reporters, outright missionaries, evangelists, or smugglers, they all should have just one purpose: to make Jesus Christ known in all nations by every possible means. We have no right to deny any person a chance to come to the knowledge of Jesus Christ as Savior. No government has the right to restrict any believer, whether in the West or in Communist countries, from traveling and making God's Word known.

I repeat: *no government has a right to restrict Christian believers from making Christ known.* That is the issue today. Are we going to obey God or men?

When God has done something on which the salvation of the whole world depends, and He has made it known to me, then I have only one duty: to proclaim it, to live it, and to be utterly intolerant of everything that tries to obscure, ignore, or explain away the great commission He has entrusted to me. That includes the distribution of the Bible which we at Open Doors think is essential to growth in the Lord and the understanding of His ways.

Where is our holy indignation, our intolerance toward any system, political or religious, that tries to prevent the carrying out of the Great Commission? We must resist such a system, we must overcome it; we must break every law that is aimed at frustrating the plan of God. I am determined to do only one thing: to do the will of God, whatever that entails.

John R. Mott, a great Christian statesman of a past generation, who for many years headed the Student Volunteer

Movement for Foreign Missions, wrote a book called *The Evangelization of the World in This Generation*. He argued along the same line:

> If men are to be saved, they must be saved through Christ. The Word of God sets forth the conditions of salvation. God has chosen to have these conditions made known through human agencies. The universal capability of men to be benefited by the gospel, and the ability of Christ to satisfy men of all races and conditions, emphasizes the duty of Christians to preach Christ to every creature....
>
> To have a Savior who alone can save from the guilt and power of sin imposes an obligation of the most serious character. We received the knowledge of the gospel from others, but not in order to appropriate it for our own exclusive use. It concerns all men. Christ tasted death for all men. He wishes the good news of His salvation made known to every creature. All nations and races are one in God's intention, and therefore equally entitled to the gospel. The Christians of today are simply trustees of the gospel and in no sense sole proprietors. Every Indian, every Chinese, every South Sea Islander has as good a right to the gospel as anyone else; and as a Chinese once said to Robert Stewart, we break the eighth commandment (Thou shalt not steal) if we do not take it to him.... What a wrong against mankind to keep the knowledge of the mission of Christ to men from two-thirds of the race!
>
> If all men need the gospel, if we owe the gospel to all men, if Christ has commanded us to preach to every creature, it is unquestionably our duty to give all people in our generation an opportunity to hear the gospel. To know our duty and to do it not is sin.[1]

Mott's fervent argument suggests that completing the Great Commission requires the efficient discipling of the nations. To do that, believers need Bibles, the whole counsel and Word of God.

Scripture everywhere assumes we have an obligation to be diligent in our efforts. We have no greater example of that than the willingness of the apostle Paul to give up everything for the sake of the gospel. (Note especially Paul's statement of strategy in I Cor. 9:16–23.)

Inefficient or incomplete obedience to the Great Commission does not count as obedience at all; our aim must be God's aim. Christians must run to attain the victor's prize. The Lord operates on a principle that increase is given to the diligent, but the slothful are deprived (Luke 19:17–26). If we know a more effective way to carry forward the Great Commission and refrain from it, then we are disobedient to the one who commissioned the church to make disciples of all nations, teaching them to obey whatsoever He commanded them.

That's why I become disappointed with some of my friends who say it is not right to smuggle when we have not exhausted all legal possibilities. How many condemned men have died while their lawful cases were still pending in the courts? Indifferent Christians in the West could condemn whole generations of people living under restriction to eternal death through their apathy.

When we talk about the Great Commission in terms of discipling, I believe there can be no doubt that having the written Scriptures is a far superior way to follow Christ than to depend on the occasional teaching of someone who may seldom see a Bible. If you would examine closely the life of Mohammed, the founder of Islam, you will discover he was eager to know more about God, but had only partial knowledge of Jewish and Christian truths, which apparently reached him only in oral form. The result was a religion that is one of the most difficult barriers the true gospel ever encountered.

131

Is Life So Dear?

Scripture itself everywhere assumes that God's people have and study the Word of God. Because the Bible has such a central role in the Christian life, discipling the nations for Christ depends upon our getting the Bible into the hands of believers in every nation.

A truly indigenous church in any land depends on the Bible being available there. Only with the Bible can Russian or Chinese Christians build their own faith, not echoing missionary concepts, but forging their own unique scriptural armor from the raw material of the Word. The Bible requires no assistance to do its work. It needs no missionary, no pastor, no explanation. It is itself the best possible evangelist, because God knows better than any human agent how Africans or Asians or Russians will see Jesus Christ and His kingdom. If we are only successful in getting the Bible into all parts of the world, the church can survive under any regime, even if all pastors are chased away and the church buildings closed.

Josef Korbel, a Salvation Army officer imprisoned in Czechoslovakia for his ministerial activities there, told me this story. One afternoon, while he was in prison, his wife managed to smuggle a sandwich into his cell. He waited until late at night to open the small package and found, between the two pieces of bread, a small New Testament. Korbel's cell mate was a madman who could not even make human sounds. He had been put in the cell with Korbel to break the Christian's spirit. When he received the smuggled Testament, Korbel began to read it aloud to his insane cell mate, a little each day, and over the next few weeks watched in amazement as the man came to his senses. He was literally healed—and brought to salvation—purely by the power of the Word of God![2]

The Chinese and Russian Communists seem to understand the value of the Bible more than we do; they are so determined to stop it. They fight the Bible more than anything else and, more than anything else, believers in those areas ask for the Scriptures. A group of Ugandan ministers in Kampala told me, while Idi Amin was still in power, "There has never been a greater hunger for the Bible in Uganda than now. The demand is increasing. Even the Russians and other Communist visitors here in Uganda come to us secretly to ask for Bibles."

Another Christian brother who operates a regular bookstore in an African country where the flow of Christian literature has been shut off, says, "Christians come to me and ask, 'Can you get me a Bible or a Christian book?' and I have to say that I can do nothing for them. They will say, 'I'll take anything, if you can get it for me.' "

Why must we be in chains before we will love the Bible and appreciate it as God's great gift to us? *Time* magazine (March 12, 1973) reported that American prisoners-of-war in Vietnam found that remembering verses from the Bible was one of the strongest bonds among them. One of their major projects in the "Hanoi Hilton" prison was to construct a Bible from memory; anyone who could recall a Scripture passage contributed. It seems people always turn to God's Word when they have nothing left.

Millions of people today have no Bibles available to them. Approximately two thousand tribes and other language groups in the world today do not have a single verse of Scripture in their own language. (Such groups are the particular target of Wycliffe Bible Translators.) In Russia alone, one-hundred language groups have no Scripture in their language, and until recently, there was a country in Europe that had no Scripture either: Albania. Almost two thousand years ago the apostle Paul was there, but to this day we still haven't prepared a Bible for Albania. No wonder the government could close all the churches, kill or imprison the few Christian leaders there, and heavily repress all signs of religion.

Only if we extensively distribute the Word of God will we have revival. Once again even governments will learn the fear of the Lord. Then the Word will end divisions among us; for we will tremble at His Word which forbids such things.

Our unconventional methods of Bible distribution have caused concern over our ethics. But is the delivery of Bibles an ethical issue or is it a loyalty issue? The marching orders of Jesus Christ demand top priority even in the face of border barriers. The Great Commission is a teaching commission based on the Bible as the text of instruction. People have to have the Bible if they are going to obey it.

I understand those who argue the end does not justify the means. But it is also unethical to allow a country to be without the Word of God when Jesus has commanded us to preach the gospel to every nation. Should the citizens of any country miss heaven because the frontiers of their country are closed to the Word of God? To cooperate with Marxist states by not violating their borders is to aid in the suppression of the gospel.

The English-speaking world received its Bible because William Tyndale decided to smuggle it in. Tyndale was so convinced of the importance for people to read the Bible in their own language he was willing to face severe persecution. In fact, he was forced to complete the translation in exile, and then smuggled it from the continent back to England.

The matters I have discussed here are most meaningful to Christians who are struggling for Christ in their own places of service, but who long to hear about the prospering of His cause elsewhere. Such brothers and sisters will take courage from the evidence in our mission that God's promises can be trusted totally, despite criticism from our friends and determined opposition from the enemy.

We do what we do in the way we do it because we believe with all our hearts that it is right before the Lord. No Christian should serve Christ on any other basis.

Should We Smuggle Bibles?

The controversy that has developed around taking Bibles into restricted countries is partly due to the very character of such work. There is bound to be some mystery, and consequently some misunderstanding, because we simply cannot describe everything about a work that requires a degree of secrecy in order to survive and function effectively. We respect the earnestness of many of our critics, and commend the way they challenge us.

At the same time, we ask for their understanding of our position, which is simply that we don't believe our Lord is willing for His Word and witness to be kept out of any country by guarded boundaries or government decrees. In fact, doesn't it make sense, in terms of work for the kingdom, to concentrate on those places that are trying hardest to keep the gospel out, and therefore must be of greatest concern to Satan himself?

Sometimes when people try to argue with me about this, I ask them what they think of the work of Trans World Radio, Far East Broadcasting Company, or other radio missions that beam the gospel into Communist countries. They say they are in favor of all of that. But what is the difference? Atheistic governments are just as much against the gospel being broadcast through the air as they are against its being carried in by car or taken in personally.

In principle, the two are the same. Both means are effective, both have to be done, and for both we need dedicated people. Even though an invasion by the gospel is illegal, as far as any totalitarian governments are concerned, it is a very dangerous thing for us to apply a double standard of morality to vital Christian efforts that have to work under restrictive conditions.

Dr. Dotsenko, the Russian scientist who defected to Canada, was asked what could be done for Christians in the Soviet Union and what he thought of Bible smuggling. He made this somewhat startling answer: "Do everything that your conscience, your courage, and your trust in God allows you to do. Shall we submit ourselves to this godless force or shall we follow the commandments of our Lord, 'Feed my sheep' ?"

Then he made a flattering statement about our work: "I must confess that I admire Brother Andrew and his co-workers. I pray for them that the Lord will continue to keep them under His protection and inspire them for their further service. This is the true spiritual battle," he said, "where people risk their lives and personal freedom for their brethren to bring them the Word of God."[3]

I am grateful for those words and for the many other insights of this man which have been helpful to me personally. But I think his key statement, "Do everything that your conscience, your courage, and your trust in God allows you to do," is not quite strong enough! That makes the future of the world and the kingdom of God dependent on too many factors instead of on the *commandment* of Jesus Christ to "go into all the world," which we must do regardless.

With all due respect to our brother, it's not just a matter of conscience, courage, and trust in God, it's primarily a matter of obedience. We must obey, going wherever God sends us as missionaries, soul-winners, apostles, evangelists, pastors, or—smugglers.

12
Can We Stand by and Do Nothing?

My heart constrains me to say one more thing.

When I read Isaiah 42:22 I seem to see my brothers and sisters in Christ who are living under oppression: "But this is a people robbed and plundered, they are all of them trapped in holes and hidden in prisons; they have become a prey with none to rescue, a spoil with none to say, 'Restore!' "

In the above quote, for the words, "to say" substitute "to demand." With none to approach the enemy, the enemy of souls, and *demand* that he "Let my people go," as Moses demanded of Pharaoh, and as Jesus also demands of the prince of darkness, the people are lost in darkness.

Christians in the West generally are all a "silent majority," making no such demand. Spineless, colorless, passive individuals, we form a bridge over which the world of corruption, revolution, and hatred passes unhindered to corrode and curse the lives of rising generations. And in democracies there is no force to stop that flow except the power of God.

God really has to be made manifest in us. The contradiction in democracies is that we have liberty even to kill democracy. By not defending the liberties of our own families, and not speaking out for those who have no freedom, we may succeed in doing ourselves in! And in not speaking out for the persecuted church, in not taking our stand for Jesus Christ, we back the devil in his evil plans for the extermination of the church.

There is no way to avoid involvement in spiritual warfare. If we say nothing and do nothing, our very default becomes a major contribution to the triumph of godlessness. On the other hand, if we act aggressively in obedience to Christ's command and in reliance on the mighty spiritual resources which God makes available, we can see the very gates of hell give way!

Jesus is King of Kings and Lord of Lords. He shall reign forever and ever. What a destiny is ours to be marching in His train across the battlefields of this world!

Once in Israel there was a time when God was silent. The light had almost gone out. But there was still one little boy named Samuel who heard the voice of God and led his nation back to God.

One person can be so important in the plan of God! That's why we must think big. We must see God's plan in global, historic terms. God used individuals to make it possible for His Son to be born one day in Bethlehem. Up to the last minute, the devil tried to prevent that birth. That's why Jesus was born in the night, surrounded by a host of angels, who were there not just to sing to the shepherds, but also to protect the life of Jesus who had become so vulnerable as the little baby in a manger that night.

Satan uses those still in darkness. The devil used astrologers from the East to go to King Herod in order to betray the baby Jesus. Those so-called "wise men" who got their guidance from the stars went to the wrong place. Their astrology did not lead them to the stable in Bethlehem; it led them to King Herod in Jerusalem who had all the babies in Bethlehem killed in an attempt to eliminate Jesus.

The same thing still happens today. Satan still uses unredeemed men in his efforts to crush the life of Christ on earth. Today, that life of Christ is in His church, which is His Body. The devil uses revolution and persecution in one part of the world to kill the life of Christ; in another he uses affluence and materialism. Capitalism has probably killed more Christians spiritually than communism has physically. It doesn't matter how many people are killed either way by the devil. Just so witnessing stops and the church fails to multiply and to pass on the life of Jesus to people around the world.

As we go out to evangelize, we don't go just to win a few souls for Christ here and there. We are a part of that great plan of God to gather His elect, in the fullness of time, into His kingdom. Since we take part in that great plan, we need to understand our role in His strategy for winning the world.

When I see the constant, unrelenting march of communism and godless social upheaval across the world today, I think of a time when I spoke at a university in Alberta, Canada, at a meeting set up by the local college Christian fellowship. After I spoke, I opened the floor for questions and immediately two young men came from the back of the hall to the two microphones up front. Both were bearded fellows, dressed in a way that in those days marked them as radicals.

In my spirit I said a quick prayer, because I sensed they were going to cause trouble. They immediately attacked Christianity and condemned Christians as racists and imperialists, while singing the virtues of Marxism and Maoism. One would talk a while, then the other. I finally interrupted them and told them they had taken their share of the time and should give an opportunity for other students to ask questions or make statements. There were hundreds of Christian young people there, but my challenge was met with deathly silence. The Christian kids were scared! I practically pleaded with them to come to the microphone and ask questions of the Marxists, but no one moved. The two students started in again, and there was nothing I could do to stop them. They were about to take over the whole assembly.

Then, just when the situation seemed hopeless, two students, one black and one white, got up and walked to the microphones. The black student spoke first: "I am from Nigeria," he started, "I would like to take this opportunity to thank the Christians who came to Africa to tell us about Jesus Christ. If they had not come, I would not be at this university. I would still be a savage and a heathen. I would be lost forever, and I am so grateful that missionaries came to turn us away from this godless revolution." The radical beside him looked silently down at his feet.

Immediately the white student began to speak. He was a refugee from Eastern Europe. "Because of the unbearable pressure from Communists, I was forced to flee my country," he said. "I am now free in this Christian country to do all the things I could not do in the land of my birth." It was perfect. He went on to tell of communism and its repression of the people. He ended by saying, "I am glad I am in a free society where everyone can speak, including the Marxist, because in my Marxist homeland anyone who spoke out against Marxism was shot." When he finished, the crowd broke into applause, and the radical students, without a word, almost ran out of the auditorium.

What a perfect example that was, though, of a tiny Communist minority taking over a situation from hundreds of Christians—all because, for a while, no one would challenge them. Two Marxists intimidated four hundred Christians and almost succeeded—not because of their superior strength—but because of the weakness of the Christians, the silent majority. It took two outsiders, one from Europe and one from Africa, to turn things around.

This incident refutes the idea that communism is the church's number one enemy. There is a much bigger enemy than that: apathy. That is the greatest enemy. The battle can only be won by those who are willing to fight!

Because the early church realized what the real problem and the real issues were, they reacted in the right way when the apostles were flogged and released and came to report what the chief priests and elders had said to them (Acts 4:23).

Did they say, "Let's agree to their new law. Let's keep quiet. Let's migrate to some more peaceful place"? No! That is not the way for people of faith and action. When they heard the report, they lifted their voices together to God (Acts 4:24). Instead of forming a protest march or writing to the United Nations, they held a prayer meeting!

They began by addressing the one in charge: "Sovereign Lord, who didst make the heaven and the earth and the sea and everything in them..." And moved quickly on to identify the true nature of the problem they faced, "for truly in this city there were gathered together against thy holy servant Jesus" (v. 27).

Jesus was in heaven, but He was still the issue. Then, as now, those who oppose the church are fighting Jesus. They are not fighting our system, not fighting capitalism or imperialism or colonialism, not fighting Western civilization, they are fighting Jesus.

Their praying continued: "And now, Lord, look upon their threats, and grant to thy servants to speak thy word with all boldness" (v. 29).

In other words, Lord, help us to step up our efforts. We are not going to be intimidated because persecution and pressure could force us to go underground. We are not going to be pressed into hiding because they persecute and kill us. Help us to be more bold.

They also asked for reinforcement in their public ministry, "while thou stretchest out thy hand to heal, and signs and wonders are performed through the name of thy holy servant Jesus" (v. 30).

One of the last literature distribution trips I made in Eastern Europe was to Czechoslovakia, when the Soviet army invaded. A week before the Russians moved in, I had a strange feeling that somehow this would happen and predicted the invasion to a friend before it actually occurred. I was in my office in Holland when my children burst in, shouting that the television news was on with reports from Prague. I turned on a set just in time to see a live report from Czechoslovakia describing the Soviet invasion.

When I heard the news, I didn't need a prayer meeting to tell me what to do. I figured if the Russians were coming to meet me halfway, I'd better get moving!

That afternoon I loaded my station wagon with Russian Bibles and drove from Holland to the Czech border in one day. I didn't even bother to hide the Bibles, counting on the confusion which I knew I would find to get me past the border without a vehicle search. When I got to the border, there was a line of cars over a mile long coming from the other direction, thousands of Czechs waiting to get out. As I had expected, the harried Czech border patrol didn't even ask for a visa, much less check my car. He just looked at me as if I were crazy, slowly shook his head, stamped my passport, and waved me through.

Six miles past the border I almost literally ran into the Soviet army. I rounded a curve and saw two huge tanks blocking the road. A Russian soldier came to the car, a frown stretched across his face, and asked to see my papers. As I handed them to him through the car window, I prayed the prayer that I had prayed so often before: "Lord, in my luggage I have Scriptures that I want to take to your children across this border. Now, I pray, make seeing eyes blind. Do not let the guards see those things you do not want them to see." And once again God honored the prayer. The soldiers didn't even look inside the station wagon. They let me through.

Can We Stand by and Do Nothing?

Several miles farther I encountered another army division in the town of Pilzen. Somehow I got in the middle of a long column of Soviet tanks rumbling down the main street. It was a strange experience, and an embarrassing one, because thousands of people lined the streets and squares of that town, all shaking their fists angrily at the Russians. But they were a quiet crowd, dead quiet, except when they saw my station wagon with Dutch registration plates; then they began shouting and cheering. I thought, "Oh, please, don't do that. This is no time to give a warm welcome to a poor Dutchman! Not with a Russian tank five yards behind me!"

Gradually, I pulled past the tanks and was on the open road again. Every time I stopped, people warned me not to go on to Prague, which was completely occupied by that time. I arrived there the second evening.

The city was a mess. Czech citizens had turned all the road signs around and had painted over all the street names and house numbers to confuse the Russians. Hastily-made signs taunted the Russians and pointed the way to Moscow.

When I preached in church that first Sunday morning of the occupation, tanks were still grinding through the streets and sporadic shooting could be heard in the distance. Yet the church was packed with a standing-room-only crowd. During that sermon, I stressed that if you do not go to the heathen with the gospel, they will come to you as revolutionaries or as occupying forces.

I challenged the people in the church that morning to seize the opportunity to evangelize the Russian soldiers, and dumped my load of Bibles on a table in front of the church. They took them and went out to give the Soviet troops the Scriptures.

The Russian soldiers were an unhappy lot. They had been told they would be received warmly as liberating friends by the Czechs. Instead they found hostile, bitter citizens who cursed them, threw rocks at them, even tried to set fire to their tanks. They were scared stiff and totally demoralized.

Then suddenly that Sunday morning, smiling Czech people came to them, saying, "Ivan, Jesus loves you. Here's a book that tells you about it!" And they gave them Bibles in their own language. "We love you because Jesus loves you," they told the Russian soldiers. This happened not only in Prague, but in other cities to which we had sent teams.

Do you know why the Communists despise Christians? It's not just because Marxists are against religion; they also despise us because we do so little to evangelize them! The Communists infiltrate our society, but we do very little to infiltrate their society. They figure if we do not regard our religion as good enough to spread to the whole world, then it can be despised and destroyed.

But the message of Jesus Christ *is* for the whole world! If we do not fight for our brethren, if we do not stand up and speak for those who are being oppressed, if we make no personal sacrifices to reach the unreached, then our religion is not true Christianity. We might as well have revolution. Although that revolution would destroy our churches, our religion, and our Christianity, somewhere some people would survive with a little Book, and in that Book they would find Jesus Christ and develop a form of Christianity not limited by well-to-do complacency. They might not even build a church building! The early believers were not concerned with buildings. They came together in homes and in the fields and stirred all of Asia Minor and Greece.

It may well be that God will let the revolution come over free countries to destroy our man-made gods and the man-made religion we call Christianity and invigorate us to take true Christianity, in the love of God, to every person in the world.

There is another aspect of God's way that is part of the expression of true Christianity. I've commented on this in my book, *Building in a Broken World*. Nehemiah expressed it as the priority to "fight for your brethren" (Neh. 4:14). This command comes first in the sequence of concern, ahead of "your sons, your daughters, your wives and your homes." Nehemiah knew that if they would take care of their brethren, they would then together have the strength to defend their own families.

There cannot be two kinds of Christians: those who pay a price and those who do not; those who live in hardship and those who live in luxury; those who carry the cross and those who "sail on flow'ry beds of ease." Our earthly government may be benign, allowing great freedom to worship and serve God; nevertheless, if we are truly children of God, we must be willing to share the suffering of the imprisoned church. We must be willing to minister to them by suffering with them. It is not good enough just to pray for the suffering church in a perfunctory manner, as if it were merely one more item on a long laundry list of prayer requests. The Bible teaches that we can actually pray for our suffering brethren in such a way that, vicariously, we suffer *with them!* We can so identify with our brethren that we actually suffer in our own spirits.

"But recall the former days when, after you were enlightened, you endured a hard struggle with sufferings, sometimes being publicly exposed to abuse and affliction, and sometimes being partners with those so treated" (Heb. 10:32–33).

This is actually a message of hope for the over-blessed Western church. So many of us have had so much, such an abundance of liberty and comfort, that we virtually wallow in the "good life." When we hear about the terrible suffering that others endure, we feel guilty and embarrassed by the multitude of our blessings. But it is not constructive just to feel guilty. You cannot help it if you were born in a free country. You cannot run down to the nearest jail and ask the jailer to lock you up for the sake of the church. But you can ask God to so burden you with the needs of the world that you actually suffer until you find ways in which you can help other parts of the body of Christ who need what you can provide.

"As though in prison with them" (Heb. 13:3). In 1967, Maria Braun, a fine Russian Baptist believer, was sentenced to five years' imprisonment in a labor colony. We printed a report in our prayer letter, asking people to pray for her, but in March 1971, *Izvestia* published an article quoting a letter in which Maria denied her faith. She said she had been justly sentenced because she had broken the law by teaching children about Christ.

What happened to Maria Braun? If she really did denounce Christ, I think I know the reason: not enough people were remembering her, not enough people were praying for her, "as though in prison" with her.

If you had been in prison with Maria Braun, would you have given her your blanket? Would you have given her your bread? Would you have given her your Bible so she could have strengthened herself in the Lord? Would you have given her your time, your love, your prayer, so that she would have been able to withstand the terrible pressure that was on her?

If you had been in prison with Christ, surely you would have done these things for Him. But you also know that He said, "Truly, I say to you, as you did it to one of the least of these my brethren, you did it to me" (Matt. 25:40). It is disturbing to think that Maria Braun may have denied Christ because we, as members of one body, didn't do our duty.

Maria is only one of many who so desperately need our help. She is not the only one whose faith may have been destroyed because of unbearable pressures. Only God knows where those who deny Him while under heavy stress really stand. That is why we ask people to pray, not just for us, but also for the persecuted church.

Can We Stand by and Do Nothing?

If we are willing to follow Christ, then we must see the world as it is—with all its problems. Perhaps I oversimplify by saying the basic problem in the world is sin. Saying that isn't specific enough; you don't have a clue as to what you can do about it. Of course, if sin is the basic problem in the world, then Jesus Christ is the basic solution. But even saying that still leaves us wondering what to do.

In John 21, the disciples of Jesus faced the same dilemma after Jesus had seemingly been taken from them. But they knew better than anyone else that sin was the basic problem of the world, and they knew that Jesus was the answer to the problem. They knew they were to play a tremendous role in spreading the gospel, but they didn't know where to begin, so Peter said: "I am going fishing." And the other disciples agreed, "We will go with you." That was the best thing they could think to do.

How many Christians today are just like that? They know that sin is the basic problem. They know Jesus came to die for the sin of the world. But they don't know how to apply that truth in order to do something about the problem. So they just go fishing, or back to whatever their secular work might be after being stirred up to do something.

But I want you to be realistic. It would be absurd for you to say that if you cannot reach some big goal, you will do nothing. If we took that attitude, we might as well go fishing with Peter. We lack a strategy, although we may be dimly aware of a solution. We know that if the whole church of Jesus Christ could be mobilized today, we could reach the entire world with the gospel in a very short time. "And then," as Jesus said, "the end will come" (Matt. 24:14). But we don't know what God wants us to do personally.

Too often we of the Western world think we can win by spending money. We do it in our politics, and we do it with our religion. What we need most is for more Christians to have a personal sense of urgency and a strategic view of the battle as a spiritual struggle. If we only had that, it would help us greatly. But we have no sense of reality, no sense of strategy, and no sense of timing. We are fighting professional revolutionaries who work strategically. They are not panicked by failure or lulled to sleep by success. We must somehow develop the same sense of strategy they have.

I have a young friend, now a colleague of mine in Open Doors, who served for several years in Vietnam. He was at a conference of Christians in Da Nang ten days before it fell to the Communist armies, and tells me that the Vietnamese pastors spent the session discussing their "Ten-Year-Plan" for Vietnam. It was business-as-usual just as if the world were not exploding outside! They didn't have ten years; they had only ten days! While they should have been preparing the church to live under persecution, many of them were talking about the buildings they would erect in the 1980s.

There are two things I have heard all over the world when I talk about the revolution: it will never happen here, and, we *thought* it would never happen here. There seems to be no other response. In so many free countries, I have heard it stated over and over: *it will never happen here*. And in the countries of Eastern Europe, and in Asia where the Chinese-armed troops have enslaved Vietnam, Laos, and Cambodia, the line has only a single sad difference: we *thought* it would never happen here.

Let me give you a specific example of how hard it is to wake up to the true danger we face. I arrived in El Salvador with Peter Gonzalez right after a military coup. I was anxious to meet with the Christian leaders. A large group of them were present at our first seminar, but I was disturbed to find that none of them seemed to take seriously the implication of the turmoil in their country.

"Brother Andrew," said one pastor, "we know El Salvador

better than you do. There will be no problem for the church here. It will never happen here."

I was frankly disappointed, but I had heard the same response again and again—even when the world is literally crumbling around the churches. That evening, the newspapers carried the terrifying headlines announcing a "State of Siege." All public meetings were prohibited—our meeting that evening included. An absolute 6:00 P.M. to 6:00 A.M. curfew was in force. Anyone caught on the streets during those hours could be shot.

The curfew had been announced at the same time as the military had invaded the national university in San Salvador, killing scores of students and arresting hundreds more. The country was suddenly on the brink of civil war.

The next morning, a small group of pastors, visibly shaken, came to the hotel. One of the six in front of me spoke for the others. "Andrew, we want to apologize. First, because our other brothers haven't come. They feel the streets are too dangerous for them to travel. And, second, we were wrong. We said that persecution could never happen here. We can at last see the warning signs. What can you do to help prepare us for what lies ahead?"[1]

The only message that can stop the spirit of revolution is the revolution of love. We have to be involved so we don't just speak the message with words, but we also act upon the message. Our lives must speak louder than our words. Then what we live will be translated into a true identification with people; we will be living the life of Christ so they can see Jesus in us.

I foresee the total collapse of organized religion in our Western world. The only thing that will remain will be true Christianity. I think that's what has happened in the People's Republic of China. A true Christianity has emerged today from the collapse of the missionary church system. For this true church, there are few buildings, few pastors, few Bibles and no prestige. But the Christians there are the true salt of the society.

There's no political answer; certainly there is no military answer to overcoming the revolution. Vietnam gave us a dramatic demonstration of the power of a handful of people dressed in black pajamas who were determined in their goal and ideology. They had dedication and they proved one of Mao's statements: "It's not the weapons that decide the outcome of war, but the people that carry the weapons."

In our Western philosophy we place far too much emphasis on things. If only we have weapons we will win the war; if only we have money we can solve our problems. That's the materialistic lie that will destroy our Western society. Communism exalts the ideology of man, man with his ideas, creative man. That's why hundreds of millions of people during China's cultural revolution walked around with Mao's little book in their hands. Give the people an idea big enough to live for, big enough to die for, and then they will go, even barehanded, against tanks and planes and win.

This is the lesson we need to learn. If we have the people who are dedicated to Jesus and motivated with the love of God, we can win the world for Christ. But most of us are at a much different point in our Christian lives. The church of Jesus Christ needs the reminder from the writer of the epistle to the Hebrews: "In your struggle against sin you have not yet resisted to the point of shedding your blood" (Heb. 12:4).

A pastor in a church in Scotland was asked why he preached every Sunday on the same verse about God's love for the world. His answer was, "I will continue to do so until *you* also love with God's love."

I was reminded of that story when someone asked me recently, "Why do you always speak about the need for Bibles, even after you've delivered so many Bibles to a particular area?" The answer is simple: the more Bibles we bring to restricted countries, the more Bibles they want because of the tremendous amount of encouragement it brings. Revival often occurs, so new churches spring up and soon many more requests for Bibles come in.

I think Project Pearl, the delivery of one million Bibles to China in a single night, proved this point. Before Project Pearl, believers had asked for one thousand Bibles and these had been delivered. But as these first volumes were delivered, the leaders inside China realized one thousand Bibles were not nearly enough. So they then asked for thirty thousand, and these were delivered over a two-week period in what was code-named Project Rainbow. Once again, the impact of the arrival of Scriptures was so great that the next request jumped up to one million copies.

Such large requests have to be verified. Estimates of the Chinese authorities as to the total number of believers in China at that time (early 1981) was that there were fewer than one million. So we asked for more information, more preparation, more indication of real need. Then the believers inside responded with data that satisfied us they had a need and could handle that large a delivery. In fact, they were asking for only one Bible for every ten Christians.

After Project Pearl, estimates for the number of believers began to shoot up even higher—to thirty to fifty million. The church was encouraged; in many areas revival broke out, seemingly just because of the arrival of the books.

You see, it does make a difference whether or not people have Bibles. As we put Bibles into the hands of Christian leaders and believers in lands closed to us, they have more influence in stemming the tide of atheism than any "fighter of communism" on this side of the "curtain." These, our brothers and sisters in Christ, live and work on the inside. They know what they believe as they read the Word. They are the ones who are overcoming Satan "by the blood of the Lamb and by the word of their testimony, for they loved not their lives even unto death" (Rev. 12:11).

Epilogue

If, after reading this book, you still have questions, please feel free to write to me in care of the appropriate address found at the end of this chapter.

But I have a question for you too. The question is a simple one: What are you doing for the Lord?

In Matthew 25:31–46, Jesus tells us about His return. The judgment which Jesus describes there does not take place on the basis of what people have promised, but on the basis of what they have done. The passage is so moving that I am going to quote it in its entirety:

> When the Son of man comes in his glory, and all the angels with him, then he will sit on his glorious throne. Before him will be gathered all the nations, and he will separate them one from another as a shepherd separates the sheep from the goats, and he will place the sheep at his right hand, but the goats at the left. Then the King will say to those at his right hand, "Come, O blessed of my Father, inherit the kingdom prepared for you from the foundation of the world; for I was hungry and you gave me food, I was thirsty and you gave me drink, I was a stranger and you welcomed me, I was naked and you clothed me, I was sick and you visited me, I was in prison and you came to me." Then the righteous will answer him, "Lord, when did we see thee hungry and feed thee, or thirsty and give thee drink? And when did we see thee a stranger and welcome thee, or naked

and clothe thee? And when did we see thee sick or in prison and visit thee?" And the King will answer them, "Truly, I say to you, as you did it to one of the least of these my brethren, you did it to me." Then he will say to those at his left hand, "Depart from me, you cursed, into the eternal fire prepared for the devil and his angels; for I was hungry and you gave me no food, I was thirsty and you gave me no drink, I was a stranger and you did not welcome me, naked and you did not clothe me, sick and in prison and you did not visit me." Then they also will answer, "Lord, when did we see thee hungry or thirsty or a stranger or naked or sick or in prison, and did not minister to thee?" Then he will answer them, "Truly, I say to you, as you did it not to one of the least of these, you did it not to me." And they will go away into eternal punishment, but the righteous into eternal life.

So what have *you* done? Or have you not done anything? Ask God for your opportunity.

In a review of one of my books, the reviewer ends with the following statement: "Maybe not every reader has been convinced that smuggling is good, but he cannot escape the impression that it is better to bring Bibles to the closed countries in the way Open Doors is doing it, than in the way other people are not doing it."

D. L. Moody has been quoted as replying to someone who objected to his evangelistic methods: "I prefer my way of doing things over your way of not doing them."

Indeed, too many people complain about the closed doors. I'm always tempted to ask them three questions: what did you do when the doors were open? What are you planning to do once the doors will be open again? And, even more pointedly, what are you doing now? I hope you are not one complaining about a lack of opportunity. He will have plenty for you to do if you seek His will and after seeking God's will, *do* it.

Is Life So Dear?

I realize that I may be asking you to make some sacrifices in lifestyle, or perhaps in spiritual pride. Still, no one has given up anything really significant for God. If we realize what Jesus Christ did for us on Calvary, then our "sacrifices" for God are only giving back to Him what He has given to us.

However, there is always a risk involved if you take a determined stand. No change comes the easy way. You can ask any revolutionary today, any guerrilla fighter—whether in Asia, Africa, or Latin America. Revolutionaries are people with ideals. They want a different world, a changed world, and they want it quickly. They also know they will have to pay a price for it. But they believe in something they are willing to die for. That should be our level of dedication too.

Once we begin to understand God's blueprint for this world, we will know that we've got to pay a price if His plans are to become reality. That's why we speak about the need for "a revolution of love." That's why we speak about being "soldiers for Christ." It *is* a fight. It *is* a struggle. Let's take a stand for the Lord Jesus Christ. We have His Word; we'd better take it seriously.

If we break God's commandments in order to stick to men's traditions, we allow the devil to continue to rule the world. We allow atheism, revolution, and hatred to continue on their course over the world. Then violence, crime, war, and bloodshed will force the church into a corner, perhaps into hiding.

Our alternative must be to break with our lazy traditions and start keeping God's commandments. He said: "Go into all the world and make disciples of all nations." He also said: "Remember those in prison, as though in prison with them" (Heb. 13:3).

One of the most courageous Christians in today's world is a girl by the name of Aida Scripnikova. Aida belongs to the Evangelical Church in Leningrad. She has been arrested many times for witnessing, for giving out tracts, for waging a single-

154

handed war against atheism, since she was seventeen years old. What a girl! Only seventeen years old and standing outside of the anti-God Museum in Leningrad telling Russians about the love of God. I tell you there is hope for the world as long as we have people like Aida!

But she has paid a price for her boldness. Time and time again she has been in prison. At her trial, the newspapers in the Soviet Union reported the proceedings and the five charges against her. *One:* she is a zealous Christian. *Two:* she had contact with foreigners. *Three:* she received Bibles. (She had fifty-one New Testaments in her flat at the time she was arrested.) *Four:* she distributed them. That is a terrible crime under communism. And *Five*: she had not repented in spite of previous imprisonments. I tell you, she never will—if we pray for her.

When Aida was in prison, part of the time in solitary confinement for witnessing to other women there, she wrote a letter which was smuggled out. When I read it I couldn't help weeping. It was the most moving letter I have ever read in my life.

Just a couple of sentences from Aida's letter: "I have been told more than once you can believe in God but act differently. In other words, believe in God but don't obey His commandments. This is the condition on which liberty is offered to me. More and more frequently the devil has started saying, 'reject His commandments' instead of using the words, 'reject God.' But both amount to the same thing."[1]

How right Aida is. What the devil was suggesting to Aida was, "If only you were a 'normal' Christian you wouldn't have to go to prison. Why should you be so fanatical? Why should you stand on the street corners and hand out tracts when that is not allowed? Aida, don't be a fanatic; be a 'normal' Christian and you'll be all right."

Aida goes on to say in her letter, "When they told one of

the brethren at the trial that he could believe in God and live according to the Bible in heaven, but not here, he replied, 'If I do not live according to the Bible on earth, I will never go to heaven.' "

What a message!

If I, Andrew, do not live according to the Bible on earth, I will never go to heaven. His Book tells me about heaven, and it is the only Book that does so; outside of that Book I have no information about heaven and eternal life. Furthermore, His Book tells me that we must give His Word to every creature and make disciples of every nation. If I disregard the commands of God, I might as well not believe in God at all. Just as that Russian brother said, if I do not live according to the Bible on earth, I'll never go to heaven.

Dear friend, are you ready for action? Are you ready to start a revolution of love? Are you ready to lay down your life for the gospel, for Jesus' sake? Are you willing to go to prison and convert the hardest criminal there? Can God take you and use you to change His world?

My dream of dozens of teams of tourists, students, families, and businessmen moving across the borders with small loads of Bibles can become a reality. The organization which now supervises these activities is called Open Doors; and from its bases all over the world we send out many teams every year to minister to the suffering church. We work hard to weed out the adventure-seekers and irresponsible volunteers, and to train the people who are to go into restricted areas. We never take unnecessary risks. We never send people out unprepared for what they will face.

We train people to go into strange places where we don't know any Christians, and we have to find them. Veteran workers go into difficult areas on information trips to make contacts, to set up distribution systems, to find out what specific things the churches in various towns need, and generally to pave the way for the larger numbers of teams that come in with the tourist flood.

The upshot of all this is that we are getting more Bibles into controlled countries now than ever before, as well as ministering in other ways. Open Doors has become, in the free world, a voice for the suffering church.

The *Open Doors* magazine identifies many more ways in which you can help oppressed Christians throughout the world. If you would like to know more about how you can be involved in this work, write to Open Doors with Brother Andrew at the following offices:

P.O. Box 47
3850 AA Ermelo
Holland

P.O. Box 30870
Nairobi
Kenya

P.O. Box 6
Standlake, Witney
Oxon OX8 7SP
England

Boite Postale 73
67140 Barr
France

1 Sophia Road
03-28 Peace Centre
Singapore 0922

P.O. Box 53
Seaforth, NSW
Australia 2092

P.O. Box 990099
Kibler Park
2053 Johannesburg
South Africa

P.O. Box 27001
Santa Ana
California 92799

Ave. Parqu de los Pajaros # 29
Arboledas, Edo. Mexico
Mexico

Box 583, Station U
Toronto, Ontario
Canada M8Z 5Y9

P.O. Box 4282
Manila
The Philippines

P.O. Box 6123
Auckland 1
New Zealand

Dalaneveien
18a-4600
Kristiansand, Norway

Postfach 29
D-8051 Allershausen
West Germany

Notes

Chapter 2

1. James L. Johnson, "To Smuggle or Not to Smuggle?", *Christian Bookseller,* February 1971, 44.

Chapter 3

1. Brother Andrew, *The Ethics of Smuggling* (Wheaton, Ill.: Tyndale, 1974). For a fuller account of the "illegal" activities of the ten Boom family in saving the lives of Jews in Holland during the Nazi occupation, for which activities many of the family paid the ultimate price, see Corrie's own book, *The Hiding Place,* by Corrie ten Boom with John and Elizabeth Sherrill (Old Tappan, New Jersey: Revell, 1971).

Chapter 4

1. John Calvin, *Institutes of the Christian Religion,* trans. Ford Lewis Battles (Philadelphia, Penn.: Westminster, 1960), 1520.

2. Calvin, *Institutes,* 1521.

3. Billy Graham, *Approaching Hoofbeats* (Waco, Tex.: Word, 1983), 33.

Chapter 5

1. Billy Graham, *Hoofbeats,* 21.

2. George A. Derkatch and Lee Roddy, *Word of Fire* (Toronto: World Christian Ministries, 1977), 70.

3. Ibid., 80.

4. William H. Hudspeth, *The Bible and China* (London: British and Foreign Bible Society, 1952), 7–8.

5. Eugene M. Harrison, *Heroes of Faith on Pioneer Trails* (Chicago: Moody Press, 1945), 72.

6. Hudspeth, *China,* 8.

7. Ibid.

8. George A. Young, *The Living Christ in Modern China* (London: Carey Press, 1948), 244.

Chapter 6

1. Edward Venables, *Life of John Bunyan* (New York: Thomas Whittaker, 1888).

Chapter 7

1. Watchman Nee, *A Table in the Wilderness* (London: Victory Press, 1969), entry for January 10.

2. David Adeney, *China: Christian Students Face the Revolution* (London: Inter-Varsity Press, 1973), 34–41.

3. Boris P. Dotsenko, "From Communism to Christianity," *Christianity Today,* January 5, 1973, 5.

4. Peter Marshall and David Manuel, *The Light and the Glory* (Old Tappan, N. J.: Revell, 1977), 263.

5. Boris Dotsenko, "From Communism to Christianity," 9.

6. Ibid., 11.

Chapter 8

1. As told to Cindy Adams, *Sukarno, An Autobiography* (New York: Bobbs-Merrill, 1965), 310–311.

2. Francis A. Schaeffer, *A Christian Manifesto* (Westchester, Ill.: Crossways Books, 1981), 56.

Chapter 9

1. Niels C. Nielsen Jr., *Solzhenitsyn's Religion* (Nashville: Thomas Nelson, 1975), 151.

Chapter 11

1. John R. Mott, *The Evangelization of the World in This Generation* (New York: Student Volunteer Movement for Foreign Missions, 1900), 18–20, 24.

2. Josef Korbel with Frank Allnutt, *In My Enemy's Camp* (Orange, Calif.: Christian Resource Communications, 1976), 129.

3. Boris Dotsenko, "From Communism to Christianity," 10–11.

Chapter 12

1. For the full story of Peter Gonzalez and the Open Doors ministry in the midst of revolution in Latin America, see *Prophets of Revolution,* by Peter Asael Gonzalez with Dan Wooding (London, England: Hodder and Stoughton, 1982).

Epilogue

1. See Xenia Howard-Johnsten and Michael Bourdeaux, eds. *Aida of Leningrad* (Reading, England: Gateway Outreach, 1972) for more of Aida's story.

Books for Further Study

These are a few books I have read with great profit. I think you, too, would benefit from what these people have to say.

Adeney, David H. *China: Christian Students Face the Revolution*. London: Inter-Varsity Press, 1973.

Andrew, Brother, with Charles Paul Conn. *Battle for Africa*. Old Tappan, N. J.: Fleming H. Revell, 1977.

Andrew, Brother, ed. *Destined to Suffer?* Orange, Calif.: Open Doors with Brother Andrew, 1979.

Frizen, Edwin L. Jr., and Wade T. Coggins, eds. *Christ and Caesar in Christian Missions*. Pasadena, Calif.: William Carey Library, 1979.

Marshall, Peter, and David Manuel. *The Light and the Glory*. Old Tappan, N. J.: Fleming H. Revell, 1977.

Pit, Jan. *Ready for the End Battle*. Kibler Park, South Africa: Open Doors International, 1980. Also published as *Persecution: It Will Never Happen Here?* Orange, Calif.: Open Doors, 1981.

Schaeffer, Francis A. *A Christian Manifesto*. Westchester, Ill.: Crossway Books, 1981.

Whitehead, John W. *The Second American Revolution*. Elgin, Ill.: David C. Cook, 1982.

Whitehead, John W. *The New Tyranny*. Fort Lauderdale, Fla.: Coral Ridge Ministries, 1982.